KNITTING

GO FROM BEGINNER TO EXPERT WITH OVER 30 NEW PROJECTS

interweave.com

Contents

GET KNITTING!

Working from patterns   6

Gauge   10

PATTERNS

Christmas tree decorations   12

Seed stitch headbands   16

Baby blanket and hat   20

Knitted flower bouquet   24

Tweed stitch rug   28

Simple lace fingerless mitts   31

Swiss darning phone covers   34

Felted pot trio   38

Loop stitch poncho   42

Zigzag neckwarmer   45

Bobble hat cushions   48

Rudolph the reindeer   54

Intarsia iPad case   58

Cable footstool   62

Kawaii kittens   66

Lacy top socks   72

Fair Isle hot water bottle cover   76

Bulldog puppy   80

TECHNIQUES

Needles and yarns   88

Knitting basics   95

Shaping knitted pieces   115

Decorative techniques   127

Circular knitting   133

Color work   136

Finishing techniques   152

INDEX   159

Get knitting!

Knitting is the final frontier of craft for me—it's the only technique I've never really had a good go at. So I'm excited to be learning along with you in this crafty compendium we've brought together of all our favorite designers from *Mollie Makes* magazine. That lovely click-clack of needles is just a few pages away, and we've gathered all you need to know about the tools and terminology of knitty matters so you won't get yourself in knots in the wool shop.

What's your choice? Kawaii kittens or chunky T-shirt yarn footstools? We've got so much covered here you're bound to find your next cast on. Knitting is one of those life-long skills that can bring us all so much contented joy and pride. Gifting suddenly gets easy and long train journeys become treasured time with our WIP. And who could say no to that? Enjoy your new craft obsession!

Lara

Lara Watson
Editor, *Mollie Makes*

Patterns

Working from patterns

There are two main types of knitting pattern: written patterns where the instructions for making a project are written out in word form; and charts or graphs where the knitting pattern is represented as a schematic drawing. Some patterns provide both these options.

UNDERSTANDING A WRITTEN PATTERN

Designers and yarn companies all have their own way of writing a pattern. Although they look different, the same information should always be there. It is important to understand what means what before you decide on a pattern and buy your yarn. The patterns in this book include the following information.

Materials: The type of yarn the designer has used and the number of balls of each color needed; colors are coded as A, B, C, and so on to save space throughout the pattern. Also listed are the knitting needles required and any additional materials, such as buttons or zippers.
Size: The dimensions of the finished project. If the pattern provides instructions for multiple sizes, such

as small, medium, and large, then the dimensions of each of those sizes are provided.
Gauge: This tells you how many stitches and rows you must have to a certain measurement. Your gauge (p. 10) must be correct to obtain the finished size of the project given in the pattern. Some patterns may state that accurate gauge is not essential for that particular project.

Featured techniques: A list of the main techniques used to make the project, with cross-references to the Techniques chapter if you need to learn a new skill or refresh your memory.
Before you begin: A useful overview of how key elements of the pattern are worked, together with hints and tips to help you achieve a successful result. Any special abbreviations or

Yarn reference card

It is advisable to make yourself a reference card with swatches of yarn on so you have a quick reference as to which color refers to which letter in the pattern.

stitches specific to that particular pattern are also explained here.

Method: Row-by-row or round-by-round written instructions for making each piece of the project followed by instructions for assembling the pieces together. The written instructions use abbreviations (p. 8) to save space and may also refer to a chart if appropriate (p. 9).

REPEATS AND STITCH COUNTS

• Square brackets are used when an instruction needs to be repeated, so you simply repeat the instructions inside the brackets a specified number of times or to the end of the row, as directed—for example, "[k1, p1] 4 times" or "[k2, p2] to end."

• Asterisks are sometimes used in place of, or in conjunction with, square brackets. So an instruction such as "rep from *" means that you should find the first asterisk above this instruction and repeat the section of pattern from this point. An instruction such as "rep from * to *" means that you should repeat the section of the pattern between the asterisks.

• When a row involves increases or decreases, the number of stitches you should have on the right-hand needle after completing the row is given in curved brackets at the end of the row.

Stitch counts help you keep track of the shaping on projects like the Kawaii Kittens (p. 66).

ABBREVIATIONS

Knitting has a language of its own and what makes it more complicated are the abbreviations. These are used to save space because if patterns were written out in full they would go on for pages and pages. Here is a list of the abbreviations used in this book, but you should always look at the abbreviations listed in the book or pattern you are working from as they do sometimes differ. There are also no hard and fast rules as to how capital letters are used.

alt	alternate
approx	approximately
beg	begin(s)(ning)
C4B	cable four stitches (or number stated) back
C4F	cable four stitches (or number stated) front
cm	centimeter(s)
cont	continu(e)(ing)
dec(s)	decrease(s)(ing)
DK	double knit
dpn(s)	double-pointed needle(s)
foll(s)	follow(s)(ing)
g	gram(s)
in	inch(es)
inc	increase(s)(ing)
k	knit
k2tog	knit two stitches (or number stated) together
kfb	knit into the front and back of a stitch
kwise	knitwise
LH	left hand
m	meter(s)
M1	make one stitch

MB	make bobble
mm	millimeter(s)
MT	make tassel
oz	ounce(s)
p	purl
p2tog	purl two stitches (or number stated) together
patt(s)	pattern(s)
pfb	purl into the front and back of a stitch
pm	place marker
psso	pass slipped stitch over
pwise	purlwise
rem	remain(s)(ing)
rep	repeat
rev st st	reverse stockinette stitch
RH	right hand
rnd(s)	round(s)
RS	right side
skpo	slip one stitch, knit one stitch, pass slipped stitch over
sl	slip
sm	slip marker
ssk	slip one stitch, slip one stitch, knit slipped stitches together

st st	stockinette stitch
st(s)	stitch(es)
tbl	through back of loop
tog	together
WS	wrong side
yb	yarn back
yfrn	yarn forward and round needle
yfwd	yarn forward
yo	yarn over
yon	yarn over needle
yrn	yarn round needle

Note

There are some key differences in terminology between US and UK knitting patterns. US terms have been used for the patterns in this book, although UK equivalent terms are included as a reminder in the techniques section.

US	UK
Gauge	Tension
Bind off	Cast off
Stockinette stitch	Stocking stitch
Seed stitch	Moss stitch

WORKING FROM A CHART

Charts show the right side of the knitting and have the advantage that you can see what you are producing, whereas with written instructions you are often not sure what the finished result should look like until you have completed a piece of the work.

COLOR CHARTS

The charts in this book are all color work designs. Each square on the chart represents one stitch and each horizontal line of squares represents one row. The color you need to use for each stitch will be shown either by a colored square or by a symbol in the square. A key will relate each colored square or symbol to a specific yarn.

Chart rows are numbered from bottom to top, with right-side rows numbered on the right-hand side of the chart and wrong-side rows numbered on the left-hand side. When working on a right-side row, you must follow the appropriate line of squares on the chart from right to left. When working a wrong-side row, you follow the rows from left to right. Color work designs are usually worked in stockinette stitch, so all right-side rows are knitted and all wrong-side rows are purled.

On charts for working in the round, all rows are numbered on the right-hand side because all rows are right-side rows, so you would need to read the chart from right to left on every row and knit every row if working in stockinette stitch.

Photocopy the chart and mark off the completed rows as you work.

Note

Textured knitting designs, such as lace or cable patterns, can also be shown in chart form. On these charts, each type of stitch instruction, such as k2tog or skpo, will be shown as a symbol, with a key explaining what each symbol means. Symbols used in texture charts are not universal, so always check the key that comes with the chart before starting the pattern.

PATTERN REPEATS

Rather than displaying a charted design for the whole piece of knitting, sometimes a pattern will give a smaller chart showing a section that needs to be repeated to make up the complete design: this is called a pattern repeat.

Sometimes the pattern repeat is repeated across the whole width of the knitted fabric, but sometimes there will be extra stitches at one or both edges of the fabric to create a balanced design. When following the chart, you work the edge stitches at the beginning of the row, then the pattern repeat as many times as directed in the instructions, and finally the edge stitches at the end of the row.

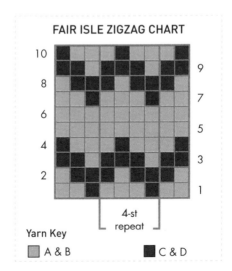

FAIR ISLE ZIGZAG CHART

4-st repeat

Yarn Key

☐ A & B   ■ C & D

The Fair Isle chart on the left is used to create the repeated zigzag design on the Zigzag Neckwarmer (p. 45).

Gauge

Every knitting pattern will give a gauge (the European term is "tension") instruction. This refers to the number of stitches or pattern repeats and rows to a given measurement. You need to match this in order for your finished project to be the correct size. By making a gauge square, you can work out any necessary adjustments.

UNDERSTANDING A GAUGE INSTRUCTION

The gauge instruction will usually read something like:
"20 stitches and 28 rows to 4in (10cm) over stockinette stitch using size 6 needles and yarn A." What this is telling you is that you must have 20 stitches across 4in (10cm) and 28 rows down 4in (10cm) of your knitted fabric.

The ball band of a specific yarn (p. 92) will also give a gauge; this is the manufacturer's gauge, based on average use. This may be different to the pattern designer's gauge, in which case you must achieve the gauge given in the pattern rather than the one on the ball band.

WORKING A GAUGE SQUARE

Using the yarn and needles given in the gauge instruction, cast on at least four stitches more than you need to achieve. Working in the stitch pattern stated, work at least four rows more than the number you need to achieve. Do not bind off: leave the knitting on the needles while you measure it. The cast on edge and the row ends may be slightly tighter or looser than the middle of the knitting, so measure with the ruler centered on the fabric rather than touching the edges.

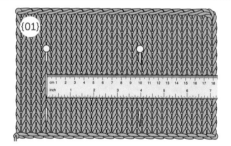

Lay the knitting flat, without stretching it. Lay a ruler across the stitches with the starting point a couple of stitches in from the edge. Put a pin in the knitting at the start of the ruler and at the 4in (10cm) mark. Count the number of stitches between the pins, including a half stitch if there is one.

ADJUSTING GAUGE

If you have knitted a gauge square and discovered you are out by one or two stitches, what should you do next? Never, ever just try to knit to a different gauge. Everyone has a "natural" gauge. If you try to knit to a different gauge, you will just end up with an uneven piece of knitting. Instead, you must change the size of the knitting needles you are using.

If you have too few stitches to 4in (10cm) on your gauge square, then your gauge is too loose and you should try again using smaller needles. If you have too many stitches, then your gauge is too tight and you should try again using larger needles.

The general rule is that one difference in needle size (p. 89) will create a difference of one stitch in the gauge. If you are out by two stitches, then you would need to alter the needles by two sizes. Continue making gauge squares until you achieve the correct number of stitches to match the specified gauge.

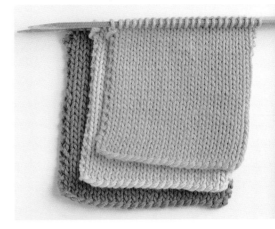

Swatches knitted with the same yarn and needle size, containing the same number of stitches and rows, by people who knit to different natural gauges.

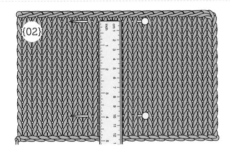

Measure 4in (10cm) down the rows in the same way.

Note

Even if you are knitting an accessory, such as a cuddly toy or footstool, where the gauge isn't vital in terms of fit, then you should still make a gauge square. This is because the style and shape of the project will be affected by the gauge. Also, the gauge you knit to determines how much yarn you use to work each stitch; if your gauge is too loose, you risk running out of yarn before finishing the project.

The gauge affects the drape and feel of the Baby Blanket (p. 22) as well as its size.

Christmas tree decorations

Bring a touch of crafty magic to your Christmas decorations with these super little ornaments. Fun and easy to knit, they'll fly off your needles in an evening. If you are a beginner, start by making the cute presents and Christmas trees, then up your knitting game with the Santa and elf ornaments.

MATERIALS

50g balls (122yd/112m) of King Cole Merino Blend DK, one in each of Royal 021 (A), Plum 905 (B), Fern 854 (E), White 001 (F), Beige 925 (G), Scarlet 009 (H), and Black 048 (I), or similar yarn (light worsted 100% wool)

Oddment of fine metallic gold yarn (C)

50g ball (155yd/142m) of Wendy Mode DK in Lime Daze 260 (D), or similar yarn (light worsted 50% wool, 50% acrylic)

Pair of size 6 (4mm) knitting needles

Tapestry needle

Polyester toy stuffing

Assorted mini pom-poms, ¼in (5mm) in diameter (for tree) and ½in (13mm) in diameter (white for Santa, red for elf)

Strong fabric glue

Red sequins, sewing needle, and thread

SIZE

Present: 2¼ x 2¼in (5.5 x 5.5cm)
Tree: 2½ x 3in (6 x 7.5cm)
Santa/elf: 2 x 3½in (5 x 9cm)

GAUGE

Accurate gauge is not essential. Work to the measurements stated in the pattern.

FEATURED TECHNIQUES

- Basic stitch patterns (p. 104)
- Increasing one knitwise (p. 116)
- Knit two stitches together (p. 118)
- Knitting stripes (p. 136)
- Sewing seams (p. 154)

BEFORE YOU BEGIN

Each ornament is made of two knitted pieces sewn together around the edges. The front and back of the tree and present are identical and worked in garter stitch. The Santa and elf are worked in stockinette stitch with different color work on the front and the back for the Santa.

You can embroider the eyes and mouth onto the Santa and elf before sewing the pieces together. However, you should add any pom-pom and sequin embellishments to your ornaments after sewing together.

The ornaments are lightly padded with toy stuffing and can be hung on the Christmas tree using a little loop made with a strand of yarn.

PRESENT

{01} Make the front and back (both alike)
Using A or B, cast on 10 sts.
Knit 17 rows or until work measures 2¼in (5.5cm).
Bind off.

{02} Make up the ornament
Using matching yarn and mattress stitch, sew front and back pieces together around the edges, leaving a gap for stuffing. Fill with a little toy stuffing and then sew up the gap. Weave in the ends.
Sew a strand of matching yarn through the center top of the ornament and knot the ends to form a hanging loop.
Wrap a strand of C horizontally and then vertically around the present and tie a bow at the top.

CHRISTMAS TREE

{01} Make the front and back (both alike)
Using D or E, cast on 12 sts.
Rows 1–3: Knit.
Row 4: K2tog, knit to last 2 sts, k2tog. (10 sts)
Repeat rows 1–4 four times more. (2 sts)
Cut yarn, thread through remaining 2 sts and pull tight.

{02} Make up the ornament
Join the two pieces, stuff and add a hanging loop as for the present ornament.
You can decorate just the front of the tree, as here, or both front and back if you prefer.
To decorate with pom-poms: Glue the pom-poms randomly to the tree (alternatively, use a sewing needle and thread to match the yarn color). When gluing, you might find it easier to hold the pom-poms with tweezers.
To decorate with sequins: Sew the first sequin at the edge of the tree, going through the hole in the sequin a couple of times to secure it. Thread the second sequin onto the needle, then take the sewing thread under the knitted stitch located immediately adjacent to the first sequin. Continue sewing on sequins until you reach the other side of the tree to complete the first row, then take your thread through the inside of the tree and up to the position of the next row of sequins. Apply three rows of sequins, then knot the thread and weave in the end.

SANTA AND ELF

{01} Make the front
Using F (Santa) or G (elf), cast on 8 sts.
Row 1 (WS): Purl.
Row 2: Kfb, knit to last st, kfb. (10 sts)
Repeat these 2 rows twice more.
(14 sts)
Work 6 rows st st, changing to G for
the third row (row 9) onward for the
Santa ornament only.
Change to F (Santa) or H (elf) and
work 2 more rows st st.
Change to H (Santa) or E (elf).
Next row: Purl.
Next row: K2tog, knit to last 2 sts,
k2tog. (12 sts)
Repeat last 2 rows five times more.
(2 sts)
Cut yarn, thread through remaining
2 sts and pull tight.

{02} Make the back
Work the back as for the front, but
do not change colors at row 9 for
the Santa ornament.

{03} Make up the ornament
Using black yarn (I), embroider eyes
and a mouth on the front piece.
The mouth is formed from three
backstitches, Santa's eyes from a
single horizontal straight stitch,
and the elf's eyes from two straight
stitches in an inverted V shape.
Join the front and back pieces, stuff,
and add a hanging loop as for the
present ornament.
Glue or sew a pom-pom to the top
of the hat.

JULIE PICARD

Julie learned how to knit with her
grandma in her native France back in
the 1980s. Now living in the northeast
of England, she picked up her needles
again a few years ago to satisfy her
obsession with bows. Julie designs
colorful and cute patterns inspired by
her love of animals and kawaii.
Visit her at www.julieandtheknits.com

Knitting Story

Knitting should always be fun and
relaxing. I love simple designs with
a cute touch, so I enjoyed making
these ornaments very much. With
a little bit of color and sparkle, you
can turn traditional knitting into
cute and festive pieces. I also try to
incorporate various techniques into
my knitting such as embroidery, and
I love using embellishments like the
tiny pom-poms on the Christmas
tree—any excuse to buy pretty craft
supplies! *Julie Picard*

Seed stitch headbands

Knit up these super bright headbands to keep your ears toasty warm all winter long. Worked in seed stitch, they'll give you plenty of practice of your basic knit and purl stitches. Quick and simple to make, your most difficult task is to decide on which to get started on first—pom-pom or twisted—the choice is yours.

MATERIALS

Twisted headband
140g ball (81yd/74m) of Lion Brand Hometown USA in Green Bay 130, or similar yarn (bulky-weight 100% acrylic)

Pom-pom headband
140g ball (81yd/74m) of Lion Brand Hometown USA in Tampa Spice 114, or similar yarn (bulky-weight 100% acrylic)

Pair of size 13 (9mm) knitting needles (for twisted headband) and pair of size 15 (10mm) knitting needles (for pom-pom headband).

Tapestry needle

Pom-pom maker or cardboard

SIZE

Each headband: 5½in (14cm) wide x 16½in (42cm) in circumference

GAUGE

Accurate gauge is not essential. Work to the measurements stated in the pattern.

FEATURED TECHNIQUES

- Seed stitch (p. 106)
- Sewing seams (p. 154)
- Pom-pom making (p. 158)

BEFORE YOU BEGIN

The twisted headband is worked as a long narrow strip of fabric that is then folded to form two circles with a twist between them. The two circles are sewn together to create a wide headband.

The pom-pom headband is worked as a wider strip of fabric that is sewn together in a single circle and gathered slightly at the seam for a ruched effect.

TWISTED HEADBAND

{01} Knit the seed stitch fabric
Cast on 6 sts.
Row 1: [K1, p1] to end.
Row 2: [P1, k1] to end.
Row 3: As row 2.
Row 4: As row 1.
These 4 rows form seed stitch.
Repeat until work measures 38½in (98cm).
Bind off.

{02} Make up the headband
Lay the knitted fabric lengthways horizontally on a flat surface. Take the two ends and fold them up and across each other to form an "X" at the center. Take the right end and fold it back over to the left. Do the same with the left end, folding it to the right. This creates the twist feature on the front of the headband (see diagram, right).
Take both ends and turn them under and toward each other so that they meet at the center to form a circle of fabric parallel with the one below. Using backstitch, sew the ends together. Sew the lower edge of the top circle to the upper edge of the bottom circle. Weave in the ends.

POM-POM HEADBAND

{01} Knit the seed stitch fabric
Cast on 11 sts.
Row 1: [P1, k1] to last st, p1.
Row 2: As row 1.
Row 3: [K1, p1] to last st, k1.
Row 4: As row 3.
These 4 rows form seed stitch.
Repeat until work measures 16½in (42cm).
Bind off.

{02} Make up the headband
Using backstitch, sew the ends together to form a circle. Pass the threaded tapestry needle through both sides, pull tight and secure. This creates the illusion of shaping on the front of the headband. Weave in the ends.
Make two pom-poms to the required size. The pom-poms shown here are 3in (7.5cm) in diameter. Use the ends of yarn from tying the pom-poms to sew them onto the headband, positioning them like a teddy bear's ears (it is a good idea to pin them onto the headband to test their position first). Weave in the ends.

KATTY HUERTAS

Katty lives in Florida, USA, with her husband and two cats. She runs her own shop, Katty's Handcrafts, where she sells chunky knitwear. Basically if she is sitting she is knitting or crafting in some way. She also spends her time painting, drawing, taking photos, and making ceramics. You can see more of her chunky knitwear here: www.kattyshandcrafts.etsy.com

Knitting Story

Since I was little I have always liked headbands, and when I started knitting they were my favorite projects as they were not very time consuming and perfect for beginners. For this project I wanted to take headbands to the next level. Thanks to the seed stitch texture they may look advanced, but in reality they are very simple to make: you just need to know the basic knit and purl stitches. *Katty Huertas*

Baby blanket and hat

It is so important to wrap up precious little people against the cold, so if there's a new baby in your life facing his or her first chilly season, get knitting this supersoft blanket and hat. Lightweight and luxurious, 100% wool yarn is a dream to knit with, and the pattern is so simple that this is a great way to take your first steps to knitting horizontal stripes.

MATERIALS

Blanket

100g balls (246yd/225m) of TOFT Pure Wool DK, one in each of Cream (A), Stone (B), and Steel (C), or similar yarn (light worsted 100% wool)

Hat

100g balls (120yd/110m) of TOFT Pure Wool Aran, one in each of Cream (A), Stone (B), and Steel (C), or similar yarn (worsted-weight 100% wool)—you will only need 20g of each color

Pair of long size 6 (4mm) knitting needles or 32 or 40in (80 or 100cm) long circular needle (for blanket)

24 or 32in (60 or 80cm) long size 10 (6mm) circular needle (for hat)

Round marker (or use scrap of yarn)

Tapestry needle

TOFT alpaca fur pom-pom or similar

SIZE

Blanket: approx 36 x 24in (90 x 60cm) after washing and blocking
Hat: *Small:* Newborn; *Medium:* 3–6 months; *Large:* 6–12 months

GAUGE

Blanket: 21 sts and 42 rows to 4in (10cm) over patt. using size 6 needles prior to washing and blocking; 18 sts and 30 rows to 4in (10cm) after.
Hat: 14 sts x 30 rows to 4in (10cm) over patt. using size 10 needles prior to washing and blocking;12 sts x 24 rows to 4in (10cm) after.

FEATURED TECHNIQUES

- Slip stitch edge (p. 108)
- Purl two stitches together (p. 119)
- Circular needle: working in rows and magic loop technique (p. 134)
- Knitting stripes (p. 136)
- Pressing and blocking (p. 153)

BEFORE YOU BEGIN

For the blanket, you may find it easier to use a circular needle to accommodate the large number of stitches, but work back and forth in rows, not in the round. The blanket pattern changes color every row. Carry the yarns not in use up the side of the work, twisting them together as you move up the edge to stop them from hanging loose, but be careful not to pull too tight or leave too loose. Slip the first stitch of every knit row to make a neater edge.

The hat is worked on a circular needle using the magic loop technique. To make the hat truly reversible, you should cut the yarn each time you change color, leaving a 5in (13cm) length for weaving in. You can carry the yarns up the fabric in a similar way to the blanket, but be aware that this will leave you with a "seam" on the inside of the hat.

Knitting Story

Knitting for a new baby is always a pleasure but never more so than when you are using a top-quality natural fiber and working a simple but effective stitch. I do not believe in spending my time making something if it is not the best I can afford. I have chosen to use pure wool yarn in three undyed natural tones. The blanket and hat have the same reversible color and stitch patterns, but as one is knitted in the round and one as a flat piece of fabric, they have different instructions to achieve that.

Kerry Lord

BLANKET

{01} Make the blanket

Using A, cast on 110 sts.

Row 1: Purl in B.
Row 2: Sl1 kwise, knit to end in C.
Row 3: Sl1 kwise, knit to end in A.
Row 4: Purl in B.
Row 5: Sl1 kwise, knit to end in C.
Row 6: Sl1 kwise, knit to end in A.
Repeat rows 1–6 until 10ft (3m) of A remains.
Bind off in A after a row 6.

{02} Finish the blanket

Weave in the ends and then wash and block.

Note

This stitch pattern will relax after washing and blocking, and this dramatically alters the size of the blanket. Although gauge may seem irrelevant in something like a blanket, it is still very important in order to ensure that the resulting fabric is as intended in relation to its density and drape, and this will impact its durability.

HAT

{01} Start the hat

The instructions are for three sizes: small(medium:large).

Using A, cast on 40(44:52) sts and divide them evenly onto the two needle tips. Using the magic loop technique, join for working in the round, taking care not to twist sts. Place marker for start of round.

Round 1: Purl in B.
Round 2: Purl in C.
Round 3: Knit in A.
Round 4: Knit in B.
Round 5: Knit in C.
Round 6: Purl in A.
Repeat rounds 1–6 three times more.

{02} Shape the crown and finish off

Repeat rounds 1–5 once again.
Next round: [P2togA] to end. (20(22:26) sts)
Next round: Purl in B.
Next round: Purl in C.
Next round: Knit in A.
Next round: Knit in B.
Next round: Knit in C.
Next round: [P2togA] to end. (10(11:13) sts)
Cut yarn, thread through remaining sts and pull tight.
Weave in the ends and then wash and block. Using C, sew pom-pom on top to finish.

Note

These patterns are simple, and thus key to their appeal is attention to detail in the finishing. Occasionally in natural yarns you will encounter a knot. It is very important to NEVER knit these knots in. Instead leave them out on the edge, cut your yarn and rejoin past the knot. You will need to weave in these ends before washing, but it is well worth it to eliminate the risk of that knot coming undone in the future and leaving you with an irreparable hole.

If you twist the different yarns together and carry them up the fabric as you work, you will get what looks like a seam on the inside of the hat. If you would prefer to eliminate this, cut the yarn each time you change color.

KERRY LORD

Kerry is the founder and creative director of TOFT, a luxury British yarn company. Kerry is also the author of *Edward's Menagerie*, a book of toy animal crochet patterns. She lives with her son, husband, and dog in rural Warwickshire.
www.thetoftalpacashop.co.uk

Knitted flower bouquet

For a summer display that lasts the whole year through knitted flowers can't be beat. A great way to use up leftover yarn, there are so many other ways to use these pretty blooms. You could turn one into a pretty brooch, or sew them in clusters to hats and scarves, tea cozies, and cushion covers.

MATERIALS

50g balls (136yd/125m) of Debbie Bliss Eco Baby in assorted colors, such as White 01, Primrose 37, Blush 27, Rose 12, Burnt Orange 33, and Ruby 31, or similar yarn (light worsted 100% cotton)—you will need approx 16g per rose and 4g per daisy

Pair of size 2/3 (3mm) knitting needles

Tapestry needle

SIZE

Rose: 2¾in (7cm) high x 2in (5cm) at widest point
Daisy: 3in (7.5cm) in diameter

GAUGE

Rose: 27 sts and 35 rows to 4in (10cm) over st st using size 2/3 needles.
Daisy: 27 sts and 47 rows to 4in (10cm) over st st using size 2/3 needles.

FEATURED TECHNIQUES

- Casting on (p. 95)
- Basic stitch patterns (p. 104)
- Slip stitch edge (p. 108)
- Increasing one knitwise (p. 116)
- Knit two stitches together (p. 118)
- Binding off (p. 112)

BEFORE YOU BEGIN

Choose any yarn colors you like for the flowers. Here, all the daisy centers are made using either White or Primrose for a more cohesive display. To create a flower arrangement for a vase, insert the pointed tip of a wooden skewer into each flower when completed. The rose is made in one piece, producing a semicircle of knitted fabric that is then rolled up to form the flower. The outer (bound off) edge of the semicircle forms the outer edge of the petals. The daisy is made in two pieces, one to create a strip of petals and one for the daisy center. The strip of petals is gathered together into a circle and the daisy center is sewn on top.

ROSE

{01} Make the rose petals

Cast on 15 sts, leaving a long tail.

Row 1 (RS): Knit.

Row 2 and all WS rows: Purl.

Row 3: Kfb, [k1, kfb] to end. (23 sts)

Row 5: Knit.

Row 7: Kfb, [k2, kfb] to last st, k1. (31 sts)

Row 9: Knit.

Row 11: Kfb, [k2, kfb] to end. (42 sts)

Row 13: Knit.

Row 15: [Kfb, k1] to end. (63 sts)

Row 16: Purl.

Bind off and weave in the end.

{02} Make up the flower

With RS outermost, roll up the semicircle of knitted fabric to form a rose, keeping the cast on edge tightly rolled and allowing the bound off edge to furl outward. Using the cast on tail, stitch the base of the rose and partway up the side edge to secure. Fasten off and neatly weave in the end.

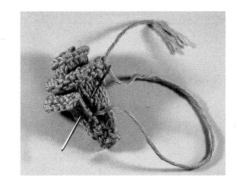

Knitting Story

Both flowers are very easy to make using basic techniques, so they are perfect for a beginner. The knitted fabric for the rose is made simply by increasing stitches. The daisy is made using increasing, decreasing, and slipping stitches. Experiment with different yarns and needle sizes for a variety of looks—for example, try a wool yarn in soft pastels. Leaves could also be added to the base of the flowers.

Sian Brown

DAISY

{01} Make the daisy petals
Cast on 2 sts.
Row 1: Knit.
Row 2: Sl1 kwise, kfb. (3 sts)
Row 3: Cast on 6 sts, knit across all 9 sts.
Row 4: Sl1 kwise, k8.
Row 5: Bind off 7 sts, k1. (2 sts)
Repeat rows 2–5 eight times more, then rows 2–4 once again.
Bind off, leaving a long tail.

{02} Make the daisy center
Cast on 2 sts.
Row 1: [Kfb] twice. (4 sts)
Row 2: [Kfb] 4 times. (8 sts)
Rows 3–4: Knit.
Row 5: [K2tog] 4 times. (4 sts)
Row 6: [K2tog] twice. (2 sts)

Row 7: K2tog. (1 st)
Cut yarn and fasten off, leaving a long tail.

{03} Make up the flower
For the strip of petals, weave tail of yarn through the slip stitch edge, then gather so that the petals spread out into a circle from the closed center. Stitch to secure the center and weave in the ends.
For the daisy center, weave tail of yarn through stitches all around edge of circle. Pull yarn tight so that edges gather together to create a raised disk for the center of the flower. Stitch the disk to the center to the daisy petals. Weave in the ends.

SIAN BROWN

Sian designs handknits and crochet for magazines, yarn companies, and publishers. She is the author of *The Knitted Home*, and has contributed designs to several other books including *Tea Cozies 3* and *4*, *Winter Knits Made Easy*, and *The Big Book of Knitting*. Sian's published work and latest designs can be seen at www.sianbrown60.blogspot.co.uk

Tweed stitch rug

Splash the color with this brilliant little rug. Made from warm and absorbent T-shirt yarn, the tight weave of the tweed stitch will keep your bathroom floor puddle free. The textured pattern is created by working increasing and decreasing techniques into the same stitches, and once you get into a rhythm, it's easy to do—you'll be finished well before bath time!

MATERIALS

Two cones (131yd/120m) of DMC Hoooked Zpagetti in Fuchsia (A), or similar yarn (bulky-weight cotton/elastane mix T-shirt yarn)

Pair of size 17 (12mm) knitting needles

32in (80cm) long size 19 (15mm) circular needle

Large tapestry needle

SIZE

17 x 32in (43 x 80cm)

GAUGE

11½ sts and 7 rows to 4in (10cm) over pattern using size 19 needle.

FEATURED TECHNIQUES

- Thumb cast on (p. 98)
- Knitting through the back loop (p. 107)
- Purl two stitches together (p. 119)
- Slip one, knit one, pass the slipped stitch over (p. 120)
- Circular needle: working in rows (p. 134)

BEFORE YOU BEGIN

The rug is knitted in one large piece. A circular needle is used to accommodate its size, but working back and forth in rows rather than in the round.

The stitches are cast on using the thumb method, then bound off on a wrong-side row to look as neat and similar as possible to the cast on edge.

The tweed stitch pattern is worked over a multiple of 2 sts. To make the rug larger or smaller, simply cast on more or fewer stitches but make sure the number of stitches is divisible by 2.

{01} Make the rug

Using size 17 needles, cast on 50 sts.
Change to size 19 circular needle.

Row 1 (RS): K1, [skpo but pass slipped st back onto LH needle and knit through the back loop of it before dropping it] to last st, k1.

Row 2: [P2tog then purl first st again dropping both sts off needle together] to end.

These 2 rows form tweed stitch pattern. Repeat until work measures 32in (80cm), ending with a RS row. Change to size 17 needles and bind off knitwise, keeping it as tight as possible.

Weave in the ends.

Four rows of pattern completed.

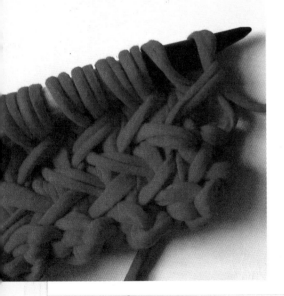

Knitting Story

The tweed stitch pattern I used for this rug design is one of my favorites. I have a thing about linking fabrics together and matching up different techniques, trying to recreate something in a different way. Combining increasing and decreasing techniques almost makes this fabric look as if it has been woven, but this knitted version is far easier to create. The bulky-weight T-shirt yarn along with big needles gives a really dense fabric and helps emphasize the texture, giving the perfect weight for a rug. *Carol Meldrum*

CAROL MELDRUM

Carol is a textile designer, author, and workshop tutor based in Glasgow, Scotland, who enjoys nothing better than playing around with yarn, coming up with new ideas, and sharing them with folk at www.beatknit.com and www.blog.beatknit.com

Simple lace fingerless mitts

These pretty fingerless mitts will keep your hands warm but leave your fingers free to keep on knitting! They are worked in an alpaca yarn, so they are soft and cozy to wear. The stitch is a simple lace stitch with no shaping involved— ideal if this is your first try at lace knitting.

DESIGNED BY SIAN BROWN

MATERIALS

50g hank (109yd/100m) of Artesano DK Alpaca in Forget Me Not C864, or similar yarn (light worsted 100% alpaca)

Pair of size 6 (4mm) knitting needles

Tapestry needle

SIZE

4 x 6in (10 x 15cm) after sewing up

GAUGE

22 sts and 28 rows to 4in (10cm) over st st using size 6 needles.

FEATURED TECHNIQUES

- Slip one, knit two together, pass the slipped stitch over (p. 122)
- Lace knitting (p. 129)
- Pressing and blocking (p. 153)
- Sewing seams (p. 154)

BEFORE YOU BEGIN

The lace stitch is simple to work by combining a yarnover with a decrease, without any shaping, so it is perfect for a beginner learning to do lace.

Unlike most gloves, there is no shaping or dividing for the thumb. These fingerless mitts are sewn up to fit your hands by pinning the seam to where you want the gap for the thumb to be. You can then try them on before sewing up to ensure the perfect fit.

{01} Knit the lace panel (make 2)

Cast on 37 sts.

Knit 2 rows.

Row 3 (RS): K5, [yfwd, sl1, k2tog, psso, yfwd, k3] to last 2 sts, k2.

Row 4: K1, purl to last st, k1.

Row 5: K2, [yfwd, sl1, k2tog, psso, yfwd, k3] to last 5 sts, yfwd, sl1, k2tog, psso, yfwd, k2.

Row 6: K1, purl to last st, k1.

Repeat rows 3–6 twelve times more.

Knit 2 rows.

Bind off.

{02} Make up the fingerless mitts

Pin out to the correct size and press under a damp cloth.

Fold one lace panel in half so that the side edges meet. Pin the sides together, leaving a gap for the thumb to fit your hand (try it on to check for fit). Using mattress stitch, sew the seam, then weave in the ends.

Repeat for the second wristwarmer to match the first.

Knitting Story

I wanted these fingerless mitts to be as simple as possible in shape, so that a beginner to lace knitting could concentrate on the lace stitch. They are rectangles folded in half, with a seam at the side leaving a gap for the thumb. They can be made to any length. This simple shape will work for any stitch or color work and they are really quick to make. *Sian Brown*

Swiss darning phone covers

With these bright, bold, colorful motifs, the phone sock has never looked so good. If you are a color work novice, there's no need to be afraid because these geometric gems are added after the knitting is complete! Swap those knitting needles for a tapestry needle and embroider your chosen design over the stockinette stitch background, duplicating the knitted stitches beneath.

MATERIALS

50g hanks (201yd/184m) of Artesano 4ply Alpaca, one in each of Cream SFN10 (A), Liquorice SFN50 (B), Anemone C986 (C), Belize 1492 (D), Bonbon SFN41 (E), and Ecuador 8774 (F), or similar yarn (sock-weight 100% alpaca)

Set of four size 0 (2mm) double-pointed needles

Four lockable stitch markers (or use scraps of yarn)

Tapestry needle

SIZE

2¾ x 5in (7 x 13cm)

GAUGE

17 sts and 22 rows to 2in (5cm) over st st using size 0 needles.

FEATURED TECHNIQUES

- Stockinette stitch (p. 104)
- Single rib (p. 105)
- Binding off two edges together (p. 114)
- Double-pointed needles (p. 135)
- Swiss darning (p. 139)
- Pressing and blocking (p. 153)

BEFORE YOU BEGIN

The body of the case is worked in the round to achieve a smooth seam-free tube of knitting, and is secured using a three-needle bind off for a neat, professional-looking finish.

The motifs are added at the end using Swiss darning, so it is easy to undo and rework the motifs if you happen to make a mistake.

JESSICA BISCOE

Jessica lives in Bristol and is a self-taught knitter, writer, and blogger. Having worked for a bank in a previous life, she now spends her time designing and teaching all things knit related. In her spare time she enjoys running, baking, and drinking tea!
www.jessicabiscoe.co.uk

{01} Make the case

Using A, cast on 48 sts. Divide sts evenly onto three needles (16 sts per needle) and join for working in the round, taking care not to twist sts. Place marker for start of round.

Round 1: [K1, p1] to end.

This round forms single rib. Repeat five times more or until rib measures ½in (1.5cm).

Round 7: Knit.

Continue in st st for a further 4½in (11.5cm).

Starting at beginning of round, arrange sts onto two needles (24 sts per needle).

Turn the work inside out and use a third needle to bind off both edges together.

Weave in the ends.

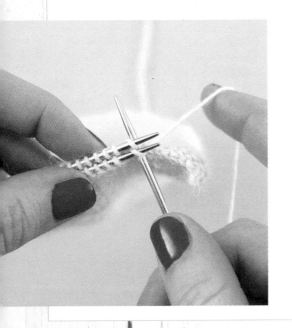

{02} Stitch the motif

Use markers or scraps of yarn to mark out an area the size of your chosen motif. All three motifs are 23 stitches wide, and 23 or 27 rows high (see charts). Using a tapestry needle and working with one color

at a time, work across the chart from right to left on odd-numbered rows. At the end of the row, position the needle to the base of the next stitch, then turn the work upside down and work across the chart from left to right on even-numbered rows. This helps to minimize long floats of yarn on the inside of the case.

It's okay to work small portions of the chart at a time, but just be sure to count the stitches as you go so that it slots into place. You might find it helpful to insert your hand into the case as you stitch to guide the needle, and avoid catching the back of the case with the needle.

Once finished, use an iron to gently steam the motifs to encourage the embroidery to lie flat, then turn the case inside out and weave in the ends.

Knitting Story

On a recent trip to Peru I was inspired by the brightly colored weavings of the traditional dress and decided to incorporate a similar look and feel into this design. To complement the style, I chose a vibrant alpaca yarn—native to Peru—to create a fuzzy authentic feel. To accommodate the detail of the motifs, the gauge needed to be tight, so I opted for sock-weight yarn and size 0 needles. This also helps to create a dense fabric to keep your phone safe. *Jessica Biscoe*

AZTEC MOTIF

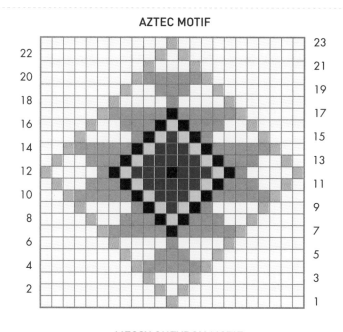

GEOMETRIC MOTIF

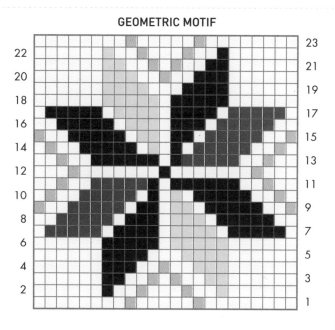

MESSY CHEVRON MOTIF

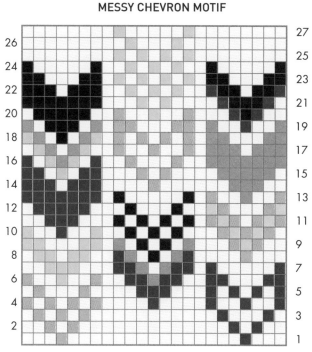

Yarn Key

- ■ B
- □ C
- ■ D
- ■ E
- ■ F

Felted pot trio

If you're a fan of textured knitting, you'll love these lumpy, bumpy pots. There are three styles to choose from and the neon-topped natural shades are a great way to disguise plastic terra-cotta. Worked in the round using double-pointed needles from the top down, there is no sewing up, leaving you more time for knitting! Hot wash to felt and the job is done.

MATERIALS

Skeins (11yd/10m) of Anchor Tapestry Wool, two in each of Green 9154 (A), Yellow 8094 (C), and Pink 8456 (E), or similar yarn (sport-weight 100% wool)

100g balls (219yd/200m) of Rowan Creative Focus Worsted, one in each of Moss 005 (B) and Natural 100 (D), or similar yarn (worsted-weight 75% wool, 25% alpaca)

50g ball (191yd/175m) of Rowan Felted Tweed DK in Stone 190 (F), or similar yarn (light worsted 50% wool, 25% alpaca, 25% viscose)

Set of four size 10 (6mm) double-pointed needles

Round marker (or use scrap of yarn)

SIZE

Tassel pot: 4in (10cm) deep x 13½in (34cm) in circumference
Seed stitch pot: 3½in (9cm) deep x 16in (40cm) in circumference
Bobble pot: 4¾in (12cm) deep x 10¼in (26cm) in circumference
Note: All sizes are after felting

GAUGE

14 sts and 20 rows to 4in (10cm) over st st using 2 ends of yarn and size 10 needle.

FEATURED TECHNIQUES

- Seed stitch (p. 106)
- Knit two stitches together (p. 118)
- Knit two stitches together through the backs of the loops (p. 121)
- Bobbles (p. 131)
- Double-pointed needles (p. 135)
- Knitting stripes (p. 136)
- Felting (p. 157)

BEFORE YOU BEGIN

Each of the pots is knitted from the top down using two ends of yarn held together, so before you start it is best to match up the end from the inside of the ball with the end on the outside. Pull a few meters together and make sure they are running smoothly.

Make tassel (MT) as follows: cast on 3 sts, then bind off 3 sts to complete tassel (1 st worked onto RH needle).

Make bobble (MB) as follows: knit into front, back, front, back, and front of next stitch, making 5 sts from one, pass first 4 sts on RH needle over stitch nearest point and off needle to complete bobble.

The pots are felted to help them keep their shape and stand up straight. You can felt by hand but the easiest way is to use a washing machine. Wait and felt all the pots at the same time if you are making more than one of them.

DESIGNED BY CAROL MELDRUM

TASSEL POT

{01} Work the top of the pot

Using A, cast on 48 sts. Divide sts evenly onto three needles (16 sts per needle) and join for working in the round, taking care not to twist sts. Place marker for start of round.

Round 1: Knit.
Round 2: Purl.
Round 3: Knit.
Change to B.
Rounds 4–5: Knit.

{02} Work the tassel section

Round 6: K2, [MT, k3] 11 times, MT, k1. (12 tassels)
Rounds 7–8: Knit.
Round 9: [MT, k3] to end. (12 tassels)
Rounds 10–11: Knit.
Repeat rounds 6–11 twice more.

{03} Shape the bottom and finish off

Round 24 and every alt round (ending with round 32): Purl.
Round 25: [K2tog, k8, k2tog tbl] to end. (40 sts)
Round 27: [K2tog, k6, k2tog tbl] to end. (32 sts)
Round 29: [K2tog, k4, k2tog tbl] to end. (24 sts)
Round 31: [K2tog, k2, k2tog tbl] to end. (16 sts)
Round 33: [K2tog, k2tog tbl] to end. (8 sts)
Cut yarn, leaving a long tail. Thread tail through remaining sts and pull tight. Weave in the ends and then felt the pot.

Knitting Story

This set of felted pots is a variation on a theme: basically, the same design worked slightly differently. Each pot is worked using two ends of the same yarn held together, and the chosen yarns are easily felted. Felting helps to keep the finished shape of the pots but also changes the character of the stitch they have been worked in. Try knitting up swatches using different combinations of suitable yarns and see what you can create. I am still amazed at what you can do with the most basic of knitting techniques and a little bit of imagination. *Carol Meldrum*

SEED STITCH POT

{01} Work the top of the pot
Using C, cast on 48 sts and work first 2 rounds as for tassel pot.
Join in D but do not break off C.
Round 3: Knit in D.
Round 4: Purl in D.
Repeat rounds 3–4 in C.
Break off C and repeat rounds 3–4 in D.

{02} Work the seed stitch section and finish off
Round 9: [K1, p1] to end.
Round 10: [P1, k1] to end.
These 2 rounds form seed stitch.
Repeat rounds 9–10 five times more and then round 9 once again.
Shape bottom and finish off as for tassel pot, starting at round 24.

BOBBLE POT WITH HANDLE

{01} Work the top of the pot
Using E, cast on 40 sts and divide onto three needles as folls: 13 sts on first needle, 14 sts on second needle, 13 sts on third needle. Join for working in the round, taking care not to twist sts. Place marker for start of round.
Round 1: Knit.
Round 2: Purl.
Repeat rounds 1–2 once more.

{02} Work the slash handle
Round 5: K15, bind off 10 sts, knit to end.
Round 6: P15, turn and cast on 10 sts, turn, purl to end.
Round 7: Knit.
Change to F.

{03} Work the bobble section and finish off
Rounds 8–9: Knit.
Round 10: K2, [MB, k3] 9 times, MB, k1. (10 bobbles)
Rounds 11–12: Knit.
Round 13: [MB, k3] to end. (10 bobbles)
Repeat rounds 8–13 twice more, then rounds 8–9 once again.
Shape bottom and finish off as for tassel pot, starting at round 26.

Note
The pots shown were felted in a washing machine for a full hot cycle (60°C/140°F). Felting is an inexact process, though, so the size of your pots may vary.

Loop stitch poncho

Your knitting granny will approve of this wonderfully soft poncho as, knitted up in a bulky-weight yarn, it is guaranteed to keep your chest warm on the coldest winter day. The deep thick pile is created using the loop stitch technique. Worked as a flat rectangle of fabric, there is no complicated shaping to do, making it perfect for beginners.

MATERIALS

Five 140g balls (81yd/74m) of Lion Brand Hometown USA in Houston Cream 098, or similar yarn (bulky-weight 100% acrylic)

Pair of size 15 (10mm) knitting needles

Tapestry needle

SIZE

16in (40cm) long at back x 59in (150cm) around lower edge

GAUGE

Accurate gauge is not essential. Work to the measurements stated in the pattern.

FEATURED TECHNIQUES

- Slip stitch edge (p. 108)
- Loop knitting (p. 132)
- Sewing seams (p. 154)

DESIGNED BY KATTY HUERTAS

BEFORE YOU BEGIN

The poncho is worked with a slip stitch edge. This helps to stabilize the edges of the loopy fabric and make them neater.

Work loop stitch as follows: k1 but do not drop stitch off LH needle, yfwd and wrap around left thumb outstretched to form a 3½in (9cm) loop (or wrap yarn around thumb more than once), yb, knit same stitch again and drop off LH needle. This creates 2 sts on the RH needle with a loop between them. Put tip of LH needle through front of these 2 sts and knit them together to secure the loop and maintain original stitch count (1 loop completed).

{01} Knit the loop stitch fabric

Cast on 34 sts.

Row 1 (WS): Sl1 pwise, purl to end.

Row 2: Sl1 kwise, [k1, loop 1] to last st, k1.

Row 3: As row 1.

Row 4: Sl1 kwise, [loop 1, k1] to last st, k1.

Row 5: As row 1.

Repeat rows 2–5 until work measures 43in (110cm), ending with a WS row.

Bind off and gently pull all the loops to tighten the stitches.

{02} Make up the poncho

Lay the knitted fabric lengthways horizontally on a flat surface, WS facing up. Fold over both ends to form a triangle shape, so that the bottom edge of one end joins the upper side edge of the other end. Using backstitch, sew together at this join. Weave in the ends.

Knitting Story

My favorite accessories are the ones that can look either very high end or casual, depending on the styling, and this cape is a wonderful example of this. One of the things that got me hooked on knitting was how much I enjoyed creating unique garments, and this poncho is definitely unique! You can customize it according to your needs, so if you want to make it even more chunky, for example, simply work a loop on every stitch rather than on alternate stitches. *Katty Huertas*

Zigzag neckwarmer

{ *Fancy exploring the world of shaping and color work? This cozy neckwarmer is a great place to get started. Shaped to a point at its base with a simple single-color Fair Isle band to frame your face, it is knitted throughout using two different types of yarn held together for a luxurious softness and warmth.* }

MATERIALS

50g balls (191yd/175m) of Rowan Felted Tweed DK, one in each of Celadon 184 (A) and Rage 150 (C), or similar yarn (light worsted 50% wool, 25% alpaca, 25% viscose)

25g balls (229yd/210m) of Rowan Kidsilk Haze, one in each of Steel 664 (B) and Liqueur 595 (D), or similar yarn (sock-weight 70% mohair, 30% silk)

Pair of size 9 (5.5mm) and size 10 (6mm) knitting needles

Tapestry needle

SIZE

12¼in (31cm) long at front x 17¾in (45cm) in circumference

GAUGE

18 sts and 24 rows to 4in (10cm) over st st using size 9 needles and A/B together.

FEATURED TECHNIQUES

- Working from a chart (p. 9)
- Basic stitch patterns (p. 104)
- Slip one, knit two together, pass the slipped stitch over (p. 122)
- Short-row shaping (p. 124)
- Fair Isle (p. 140)
- Pressing and blocking (p. 153)
- Sewing seams (p. 154)

BEFORE YOU BEGIN

This design is worked using one end of light worsted-weight yarn and one end of sock-weight yarn held together throughout. For the Fair Isle band toward the top of the design, you change to size 10 needles to keep the fabric at the same gauge.

The pattern has 3 sts at the most between colors, so you will not need to catch in the stranded yarns on the back but simply float them across.

DESIGNED BY CAROL MELDRUM

Knitting Story

I enjoy playing about with yarns and plying them together, and the combination of a light worsted wool blend with a luxury sock-weight mohair/silk mix works brilliantly. Working on a larger needle allows the blend of fibers to breathe and fluff up, creating a fabric that is nice and cozy but with a drape, while the tone-on-tone colors add to the tweed effect. I am all for experimenting, though, and I am sure this would look just as good in completely contrasting shades—give it a go! *Carol Meldrum*

{01} Start the neckwarmer
Using size 9 needles and A and B held together, cast on 89 sts.
Row 1: K43, sl1, k2tog, psso, knit to end. (87 sts)
Row 2: K42, sl1, k2tog, psso, knit to end. (85 sts)
Row 3: K41, sl1, k2tog, psso, knit to end. (83 sts)
Row 4: K40, sl1, k2tog, psso, knit to end. (81 sts)

{02} Work short-row shaping
Next row: K42, wrap next st as folls: yfwd, sl1 pwise, yb, turn.
Next row: Sl1 pwise, p3, wrap next st as folls: yb, sl1 pwise, yfwd, turn.
Next row: Sl1 pwise, knit up to wrapped stitch, pick up wrapped strand around stitch and place on LH needle, knit the strand and stitch together, k2, wrap next st, turn.
Next row: Sl1 pwise, purl up to wrapped stitch, pick up wrapped strand around stitch and place on LH needle, purl the strand and stitch together, p2, wrap next st, turn.
Repeat last 2 rows, moving the wrapped stitch by 2 sts on each row, until 8 sts remain on LH needle, knit to end.

{03} Work the straight section and Fair Isle zigzag
Starting and ending with a purl (WS) row, work 21 rows st st.
Change to size 10 needles.
Using Fair Isle technique and yarns A/B and C/D held together, work next 10 rows from chart as folls:

RS rows: Work first 2 sts of chart, [work 4-st patt rep] to last 3 sts, work last 3 sts of chart.
WS rows: Work first 3 sts of chart, [work 4-st patt rep] to last 2 sts, work last 2 sts of chart.
Change to size 9 needles.
Knit 5 rows.
Bind off knitwise.

{04} Make up the neckwarmer
Weave in the ends and then press gently on the WS.
Using yarns A/B together and mattress stitch or backstitch, sew up the back seam.

{02}

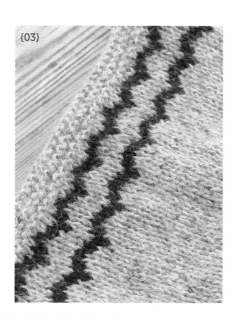

{03}

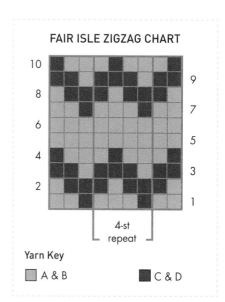

FAIR ISLE ZIGZAG CHART

4-st repeat

Yarn Key
☐ A & B   ■ C & D

Bobble hat cushions

Let your bobble hat addiction spill over into your home with these coordinating novelty pillows. Using stockinette stitch, seed stitch, intarsia, and three different rib patterns, they max out on technique but will knit up quickly in a worsted-weight yarn. Just one ball each of five colors of yarn makes all three cushions complete with pom-poms.

MATERIALS

100g balls (214yd/196m) of Stylecraft Special Aran, one in each of Pomegranate 1083 (A), Spice 1711 (B), Aspen 1422 (C), Aster 1003 (D), and Fondant 1241 (E), or similar yarn (worsted-weight 100% acrylic)

Pair of size 8 (5mm) knitting needles

Tapestry needle

Polyester toy stuffing

Pom-pom maker or cardboard

Fourteen yarn bobbins (optional)

SIZE

12½in (32cm) wide x 13½in (34cm) high excluding pom-pom

GAUGE

18 sts and 24 rows to 4in (10cm) over st st using size 8 needles.

FEATURED TECHNIQUES

- Working from a chart (p. 9)
- Stockinette stitch (p. 104)
- Rib (p. 105)
- Seed stitch (p. 106)
- Knit two stitches together (p. 118)
- Purl two stitches together (p. 119)
- Knitting stripes (p. 136)
- Intarsia (p. 149)
- Sewing seams (p. 154)
- Pom-pom making (p. 158)

BEFORE YOU BEGIN

The sides of the cushion are curved using simple decreases. When the pattern instructs you to decrease one stitch at each end of a row, work k2tog at each end of RS rows and p2tog at each end of WS rows.

Before starting the intarsia diamonds cushion, wind off several small balls or bobbins of each yarn color. You will need: 3A, 2B, 4C, 2D, and 3E. Use a separate ball/bobbin for each area of color worked. When changing color, twist the yarns around each other to stop holes from forming.

WIDE-STRIPED CUSHION

{01} Make the front and back (both alike)

Using A, cast on 58 sts.

Row 1 (RS): [P1, k1] to end.

This row forms single rib. Repeat thirteen times more.

Change to B and beg with a knit row, work 20 rows st st.

Change to C and work 8 rows st st.

Continue in st st, dec 1 st at each end of next and foll 2 fourth rows. (52 sts)

Work 3 rows without shaping.

Change to B.

*Dec 1 st at each end of next and foll 5 alt rows. (40 sts)

Dec 1 st at each end of next 7 rows. (26 sts)

Next row: Bind off 2 sts, knit to last 2 sts, k2tog. (23 sts)

Next row: Bind off 2 sts, purl to last 2 sts, p2tog. (20 sts)

Next row: Bind off 2 sts, knit to end. (18 sts)

Next row: Bind off 2 sts, purl to end. (16 sts)

Bind off.

{02} Make up the cushion

Weave in the ends. Place front and back RS together, then sew around sides and top using backstitch, taking care to color match stripes and shaping. Sew partway along bottom edge, leaving a gap for turning. Turn RS out, pushing the corners out well.

Using A, make a 3½in (9cm) diameter pom-pom. Use the ends of yarn from tying the pom-pom to attach it to the center top of the cushion, knotting the yarn securely on the inside.

Stuff the cushion well with the polyester toy stuffing, shaping it as you go so that there are no unsightly lumps. Sew the gap in the bottom edge closed.

Knitting Story

When considering the yarn for this cushion set, the available color range was my first priority, along with a slightly bulkier weight so that they would be quick to knit. I wanted really fresh, bright, and fun colors and a rounded, soft yarn for stitch definition. The yarn I chose delivered on both counts and was lovely to work with. I really enjoy designing and making quirky knits, and love knitting for the home. Who says bobble hats are just for your head! *Zoë Halstead*

SEED STITCH STRIPY CUSHION

{01} Make the front and back (both alike)
Using D, cast on 57 sts.
Row 1 (RS): K2, [p1, k3] to last 3 sts, p1, k2.
Row 2: P1, [k3, p1] to end.
These 2 rows form seed stitch rib.
Repeat six times more.
Beg with a knit row, work 8 rows st st.
Change to E.
Next row: P1, [k1, p1] to end.
Work 7 rows st st.
Change to A and repeat last 8 rows.
Change to B.
Next row: P1, [k1, p1] to end.
Work 3 rows st st.
Start shaping sides as folls:
Next row: Knit, dec 1 st at each end row. (55 sts)
Work 3 rows st st.
Change to D.
Next row: P2tog, [k1, p1] to last 3 sts, k1, p2tog. (53 sts)
Work 3 rows st st.
Next row: Knit, dec 1 st at each end row. (51 sts)
Work 3 rows st st.
Change to E.
Next row: P2tog, [k1, p1] to last 3 sts, k1, p2tog. (49 sts)
Purl 1 row.
Continue in st st, dec 1 st at each end of next and foll 2 alt rows. (43 sts)
Purl 1 row.
Change to A.

Next row: P2tog, [k1, p1] to last 3 sts, k1, p2tog. (41 sts)
Purl 1 row.
Dec 1 st at each end of next 6 st st rows. (29 sts)
Change to B.
Next row: K2tog, [p1, k1] to last 3 sts, p1, k2tog. (27 sts)
Next row: Purl, dec 1 st at each end row. (25 sts)
Next row: Bind off 2 sts, knit to last 2 sts, k2tog. (22 sts)

Next row: Bind off 2 sts, purl to last 2 sts, p2tog. (19 sts)
Next row: Bind off 2 sts, knit to end. (17 sts)
Next row: Bind off 2 sts, purl to end. (15 sts)
Bind off.

{02} Make up the cushion
Finish as instructed for the wide-striped cushion, but use D to make the pom-pom.

INTARSIA DIAMONDS CUSHION

{01} Make the front and back (both alike)

Using C, cast on 58 sts.

Row 1 (RS): K2, [p2, k2] to end.

Row 2: P2, [k2, p2] to end.

These 2 rows form double rib.

Repeat six times more.

Using the intarsia technique, start working from the chart as folls:

Next row: Knit across 58 sts of row 1 of chart.

Next row: Purl across 58 sts of row 2 of chart.

Continue in st st until all 28 rows of chart have been worked.

Start shaping sides as folls:

Next row: K2togE, k3E, k5C, k9A, k5C, k9B, k5C, k9D, k5C, k4E, k2togE. (56 sts)

Next row: P4E, p7C, p7D, p7C, p7B, p7C, p7A, p7C, p3E.

Next row: K3E, k7C, k7A, k7C, k7B, k7C, k7D, k7C, k4E.

Next row: P3E, p9C, p5D, p9C, p5B, p9C, p5A, p9C, p2E.

Next row: K2togE, k9C, k5A, k9C, k5B, k9C, k5D, k9C, k1E, k2togE. (54 sts)

Next row: P1E, p11C, p3D, p11C, p3B, p11C, p3A, p11C.

Next row: K11C, k3A, k11C, k3B, k11C, k3D, k11C, k1E.

Next row: P13C, p1D, p13C, p1B, p13C, p1A, p12C.

Continue in C only.

Next row: Knit, dec 1 st at each end of row. (52 sts)

Work 3 rows st st.

Continue as given for wide-striped cushion from * to end.

{02} Make up the cushion

Weave in the ends, tightening any holes that have appeared between yarn changes.

Finish as instructed for the wide-striped cushion, but use E to make the pom-pom.

ZOË HALSTEAD

Zoë was taught to knit at the age of five by her gran. Having tried her hand at, and enjoyed, most needlecrafts through the years, knitting will always remain her first love. Zoë has written needlecraft books and designs for magazines and yarn companies. Visit her blog to find out more and say hello: www.zoesneedles.wordpress.com

INTARSIA DIAMONDS CUSHION

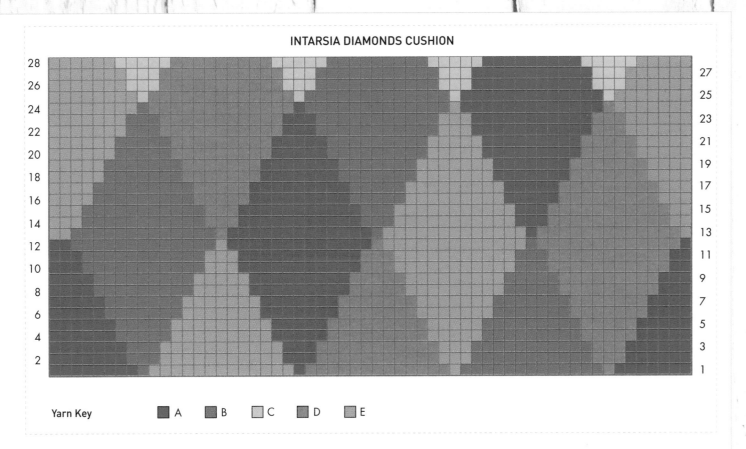

Yarn Key	■ A	■ B	☐ C	■ D	■ E

Before working the intarsia diamond pattern, wind small amounts of yarn onto bobbins for each area of color. This will help keep the yarns organized and reduce the risk of tangling.

Rudolph the reindeer

This knitted Rudolph is meant for a hanging wall display, but as he is filled with supersoft polyester stuffing, he doubles up as a great cushion or bedtime pal, too—but do use safety buttons for eyes if you make him for a child. Using a silky yarn for his nose makes him just that little bit more special—you won't be able to resist tweaking it every time you go past!

MATERIALS

50g balls (93yd/85m) of Rico Design Creative Cotton Aran, two in Nougat 56 (A) and one in Brown 58 (B), or similar yarn (worsted-weight 100% cotton)

100g ball (236yd/216m) of King Cole Smooth DK in Cherry 829 (C), or similar yarn (light worsted 100% microfiber)

Pair of size 6 (4mm) knitting needles

Four stitch holders

Pom-pom maker or cardboard

Tapestry needle

8oz (250g) bag of polyester toy stuffing

³/₈in (9mm) black beads for eyes, and sewing needle and black thread

SIZE

9in (23cm) at widest point x 16in (40cm) high including antlers

GAUGE

Accurate gauge is not essential for this pattern.

FEATURED TECHNIQUES

- Make one (p. 115)
- Increasing one knitwise (p. 116)
- Knit two stitches together (p. 118)
- Knit two stitches together through the backs of the loops (p. 121)
- Sewing seams (p. 154)
- Pom-pom making (p. 158)

BEFORE YOU BEGIN

Rudolph's head is worked as two flat pieces and then stitched together and stuffed.

Each antler is worked as a single piece of knitting. The branches are created by separating some of the stitches onto stitch holders, and then working on different groups of stitches one at a time to create the three points of the antlers.

{01} Make the front and back of the head (both alike)

Using A, cast on 20 sts.

Row 1 and all WS rows: Purl.

Row 2 (RS): [K1, kfb] to end. (30 sts)

Row 4: [K2, kfb] to end. (40 sts)

Row 6: K4, [kfb, k9] 3 times, kfb, k5. (44 sts)

Row 8: K4, kfb, k10, kfb, k11, kfb, k10, kfb, k5. (48 sts)

Row 10: K4, kfb, k11, kfb, k13, kfb, k11, kfb, k5. (52 sts)

Row 12: K4, kfb, k12, kfb, k15, kfb, k12, kfb, k5. (56 sts)

Row 14: Knit.

Row 16: K18, kfb, k17, kfb, k19. (58 sts)

Work 19 rows st st.

Row 36: K8, k2tog tbl, knit to last 10 sts, k2tog, k8. (56 sts)

Row 38: K7, k2tog tbl, knit to last 9 sts, k2tog, k7. (54 sts)

Row 40: K6, k2tog tbl, knit to last 8 sts, k2tog, k6. (52 sts)

Row 42: K5, k2tog tbl, k12, k2tog tbl, k10, k2tog, k12, k2tog, k5. (48 sts)

Row 44: K4, k2tog tbl, k11, k2tog tbl, k10, k2tog, k11, k2tog, k4. (44 sts)

Row 46: K3, k2tog tbl, k10, k2tog tbl, k10, k2tog, k10, k2tog, k3. (40 sts)

Row 48: K2, k2tog tbl, k9, k2tog tbl, k10, k2tog, k9, k2tog, k2. (36 sts)

Row 50: K11, k2tog tbl, k10, k2tog, k11. (34 sts)

Work 25 rows st st.

Row 76: K9, k2tog tbl, k12, k2tog, k9. (32 sts)

Row 78: K8, k2tog tbl, k12, k2tog, k8. (30 sts)

Row 80: K7, k2tog tbl, k12, k2tog, k7. (28 sts)

Row 82: K6, k2tog tbl, k12, k2tog, k6. (26 sts)

Row 84: K5, k2tog tbl, k12, k2tog k5. (24 sts)

Bind off purlwise.

{02} Make the antlers (make 2)

Using B, cast on 15 sts.

Row 1 and all WS rows: Purl.

Row 2 (RS): Purl.

Row 4: K2, M1, knit to last 2 sts, M1, k2. (17 sts)

Row 6: K3, M1, knit to last 3 sts, M1, k3. (19 sts)

Row 8: K4, M1, knit to last 4 sts, M1, k4. (21 sts)

Row 10: K5, M1, knit to last 5 sts, M1, k5. (23 sts)

Row 12: K6, M1, knit to last 6 sts, M1, k6. (25 sts)

Row 13: Cut yarn and place first 6 sts onto a stitch holder, rejoin yarn to rem sts and p13, place last 6 sts onto another stitch holder.

Row 14: Knit.

Repeat rows 3–12 once more. (23 sts)

Row 25: Cut yarn and place first 6 sts onto a stitch holder, rejoin yarn to rem sts and p11, place last 6 sts onto another stitch holder.

Work 6 rows st st.

Row 32: [K2tog] to last st, k1. (6 sts)

Cut yarn, thread through remaining 6 sts and pull tight.

*Place sts from first pair of stitch holders onto LH needle with WS facing.

Starting with a purl row, work 7 rows st st across all 12 sts.

Next row: [K2tog] to end. (6 sts)

Cut yarn, thread through remaining 6 sts and pull tight.

Repeat from * for stitches on second pair of stitch holders, but only work 5 rows st st.

Knitting Story

As an interior designer, I am fascinated by the continuing trend for taxidermy in the home. While there are hundreds of beautiful high street styles ranging from the cute to the downright weird, being a huge animal lover I always feel slightly uneasy about them. It therefore made perfect sense to make a "kind" taxidermy design using my favorite skill of knitting. I opted for a gorgeous natural cotton yarn for the head and antlers, and used a slightly lustrous smooth yarn to get a really shiny nose as only Rudolph has! *Julia Groves*

{03) Make the nose

Using C, make a 2½in (6cm) diameter pom-pom. Once you think you have enough yarn threaded around the pom-pom maker, do an extra couple of rounds for a really densely packed pom-pom. When tying the pom-pom, leave long tails of yarn for sewing it to the head.

{04) Make up the reindeer

Using matching yarn and mattress stitch, sew front and back of head together, leaving a gap for stuffing. Stuff until softly full, then sew up the gap.

Join side seams of antlers together, then stuff firmly. Sew cast on edge of antlers to top of head.

Sew the pom-pom nose to the head, centered in the bottom fifth of the reindeer's face.

Sew the eyes in place, centered under the antlers or wherever you feel they look best.

JULIA GROVES

Over the past 20 years Julia has built up an enviable reputation as an interior designer, creative director, and product designer. Her work regularly features in newspapers, magazines, and across television and radio. Rupert's House is the culmination of these years of experience, offering handmade homewares with a modern design made using traditional skills.
www.rupertshouse.etsy.com

Intarsia iPad case

Make sure your iPad stays nice and secure with this simple to make zip-up case. The front panel, knitted using intarsia with a little bit of Fair Isle thrown in for luck, is a great way to build on your color work techniques. The back panel is made from faux leather fabric to help keep the shape of the case, providing maximum protection for your prized possession.

MATERIALS

100g ball (273yd/250m) of Jarol Heritage DK in Kingfisher 136 (A), or similar yarn (light worsted 55% wool, 25% acrylic, 20% nylon)

25g ball (109yd/100m) of Twilley's Goldfingering in Gold 02 (B), or similar yarn (light worsted 80% viscose, 20% metallic polyester)

Pair of size 6 (4mm) knitting needles

Tapestry needle

10in (25cm) dress zipper

12 x 9in (30 x 23cm) piece of faux leather or any heavy, stiff wool or felted fabric of your choice

Sewing thread in turquoise or color to match your case

Sewing machine or sewing needle (suitable for leather if using)

SIZE

11 x 8¼in (28 x 21cm)

GAUGE

22 sts and 28 rows to 4in (10cm) over st st using size 6 needles and A.

FEATURED TECHNIQUES

- Working from a chart (p. 9)
- Basic stitch patterns (p. 104)
- Fair Isle (p. 140)
- Intarsia (p. 149)

BEFORE YOU BEGIN

The gold thought clouds are worked using the intarsia technique. Wind off a separate ball or bobbin of yarn for each section of color and twist the yarn at the back of the work to avoid creating holes.

The blue @ symbol is knitted using the Fair Isle technique. This saves lots of swapping yarn bobbins.

When working the Fair Isle section, carry the yarn loosely across the back of the work and never over more than 7 sts without catching it in on the reverse. For the neatest result, you should catch in the yarn on the reverse of the work whenever you are stranding it across more than 3 sts.

Hold yarn B double throughout.

Knitting Story

My first thoughts on designing an iPad/tablet case were based around technology and the internet, and I eventually settled on the @ symbol—where would we be without it? It is mainly worked using the intarsia technique, with a little Fair Isle where the @ symbol is knitted in. I could not resist using gold yarn—it's my favorite—but I would encourage you to play around with color and yarn combinations to create something you love. **Rebecca Rymsza**

{01} Make the front panel

Using A, cast on 65 sts.

Work 10 rows st st.

Using the intarsia and Fair Isle techniques, start working from chart as folls:

Row 1 (RS): K51A, join in two ends of B held together and k2B, k12A.

Row 2: P11A, p4B, purl to end in A.

Continue in st st until all 48 rows of chart have been worked.

Work 5 rows st st in A.

Bind off and weave in the ends.

{02} Make up the case

With RS together and edges aligned, pin the zipper along one long side of the leather fabric and weave in place. Repeat to attach the other edge of the zipper to the top of the knitted front piece. Open the zipper halfway.

Pin around the other three sides of the leather and knitted fabric and sew together. Weave in the ends. Open the zipper fully and turn the case RS out.

REBECCA RYMSZA

Rebecca is founder and knitter-in-chief at WMJ. WMJ knits bespoke sweaters and introduces talented knitwear graduates and emerging designers via its online shop and magazine, both of which can be found at www.wearewmj.com. Rebecca likes knitting, Paris, *The Sopranos*, her apartment in the city, walks in the country, and anything that glitters.

The colors are carried across the back of the @ symbol using the Fair Isle technique. The remainder of the design is worked using the intarsia method.

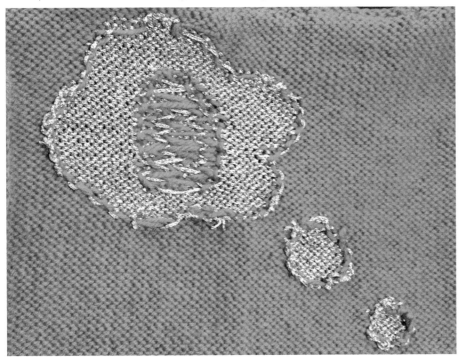

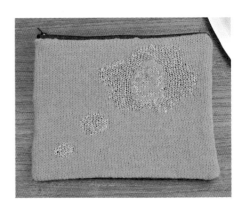

THOUGHT CLOUD CHART

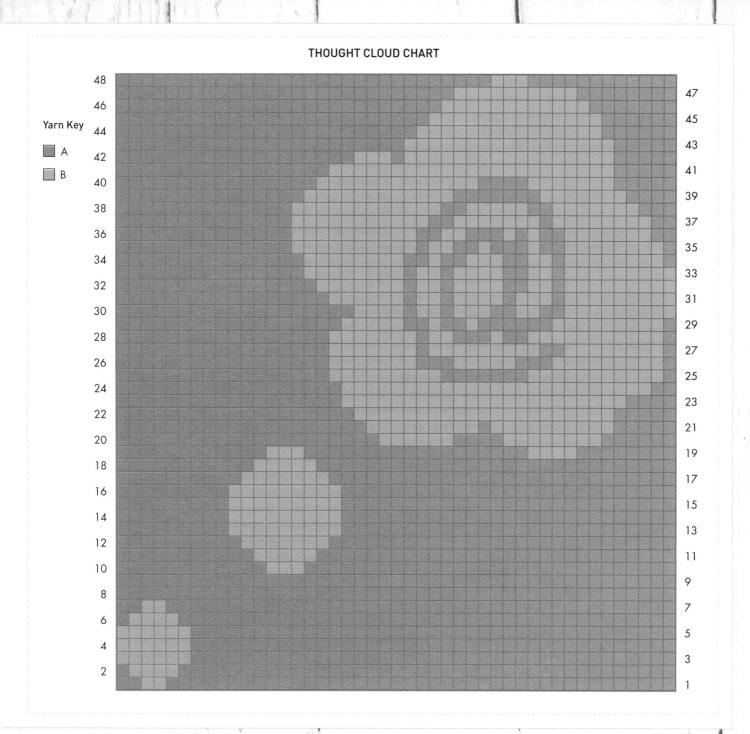

Yarn Key

A

B

Cable footstool

This richly textured footstool is worked using super-sized T-shirt yarn, a recycled by-product of the fashion industry, so you can feel eco-friendly while you knit. The cable pattern around the middle is the perfect introduction to cabling—a technique that looks impressive but is surprisingly easy to do—and the smooth fabric yarn shows off the stitch pattern beautifully.

MATERIALS

Three cones (131yd/120m) of DMC Hoooked Zpagetti in Marina, or similar yarn (bulky-weight cotton/elastane mix T-shirt yarn)

Two 32in (80cm) long size 17 (12mm) circular needles

Cable needle

Large tapestry needle

Jersey fabric tube or pillowcase (it doesn't matter which but it has to be a stretchy fabric) in a color to complement your choice of yarn

Two elastic bands (optional)

Approx 40oz (1250g) polyester toy stuffing

SIZE

16in (40cm) high x 59in (150cm) in circumference

GAUGE

10 sts and 9½ rows to 4in (10cm) over cable pattern using size 17 needles.

8 sts and 12 rows to 4in (10cm) over garter stitch using size 17 needles.

FEATURED TECHNIQUES

- Garter stitch (p. 104)
- Slip stitch edge (p. 108)
- Short-row shaping (p. 124)
- Cables (p. 127)
- Circular needle: working in rows (p. 134)
- Sewing seams (p. 154)

BEFORE YOU BEGIN

Use the two circular needles just like a pair of straight needles, knitting back and forth in rows.

The footstool is knitted sideways on using the short-row technique—stopping before the end of the row so more rows are worked in the middle of the knitting than at the edges—to give the footstool its rounded shape.

The sides are worked with a slip stitch edge, making it easy to gather the edge into a tight circle to form the top and bottom of the footstool.

Work C4B (cable 4 back) as follows: slip 2 sts onto cable needle and hold at back of work, knit next 2 sts on LH needle, then knit 2 sts from cable needle.

Work C4F (cable 4 front) as follows: slip 2 sts onto cable needle and hold at front of work, knit next 2 sts on LH needle, then knit 2 sts from cable needle.

{01} Knit the cable panel

Cast on 54 sts.

Row 1 (RS): K19, [p1, k4] 3 times, p1, k19.

Row 2: K20, [p4, k1] 3 times, k19. These 2 rows set the position of the cables and garter st edges.

Row 3: Sl1 pwise, tighten st on needle, yb, k18, p1, C4F, p1, k4, p1, C4F, p1, k13, turn.

Row 4: Sl1 pwise, tighten st on needle, yb, k13, [p4, k1] 3 times, k13, turn.

Row 5: Sl1 pwise, tighten st on needle, yb, k12, p1, k4, p1, C4B, p1, k4, p1, k6, turn.

Row 6: Sl1 pwise, tighten st on needle, yb, k6, [p4, k1] 3 times, k6, turn.

Row 7: Sl1 pwise, tighten st on needle, yb, k5, [p1, k4] 3 times, p1, k19 to end.

Row 8: Sl1 pwise, tighten st on needle, yb, k19, [p4, k1] 3 times, k19 to end.

Rows 3–8 set cable patt and short-row sequence. Repeat 23 times more or until work measures 59in (150cm) around the central cable. Bind off evenly in patt, leaving long tail of yarn for making up.

{02} Make up the footstool

Thread yarn tail through a large tapestry needle and weave through every other slipped stitch along one side edge of the panel. Pull up to gather the edge into a tight circle and sew through the stitches several times to secure.

Sew the cast on and bound off edges together, leaving the other side edge as an opening at the top of the footstool for stuffing.

{03} Stuff the footstool

Either knot or use an elastic band to gather and fasten one end of the jersey tube or pillowcase. Place some stuffing inside and push down to form a flat base. Place the partially stuffed jersey fabric inside the knitted footstool and push well down into the base.

Add more stuffing, making sure to push the central cable section outward to form a nice rounded shape. Once you are satisfied that the footstool is well stuffed, fasten an elastic band around the top of the jersey and push the remaining fabric down inside the knitted outer. Thread a length of yarn onto the tapestry needle and gather up the top edge of the footstool as before. Sew through the stitches several times to secure and fasten off. Weave in the end.

Knitting Story

When I first cast on this project and began knitting it, I did so using straight needles. I found it hard on my hands and I was not able to knit in my usual way because the yarn is quite heavy and stretchy. I switched to using two circular needles and this was a lot easier, plus it allowed me to check the shape of the footstool better as it naturally curved around. Also, don't be surprised if the yarn varies in thickness—mine did a lot! *Zoë Halstead*

Kawaii kittens

These fast food kittens are a trio of kawaii-inspired cuteness, with a side order of stuffing, eyes, and whiskers! Knitted up in two identical pieces and sewn together, they are a perfect project if you are looking to improve your basic knitting skills. Start with the Ice Cream or Burger Kitten, and then for a color challenge try the Popcorn Kitten.

MATERIALS

For details of yarns used, refer to the method for each kitten on the following pages

Pair of size 6 (4mm) knitting needles

Stitch holder

Tapestry needle

Polyester toy stuffing

Black toy safety eyes, ⅜in (10mm) in diameter, with washers

Black felt for nose and whiskers

Sewing needle and black thread, or strong fabric glue

SIZE

7in (18cm) at widest point x 7in (18cm) high excluding ears

GAUGE

22 sts and 30 rows to 4in (10cm) over st st using size 6 needles.

FEATURED TECHNIQUES

- Long tail cast on (p. 99)
- Increasing one knitwise (p. 116)
- Decreasing (pp. 118, 119 and 120)
- Color work (pp. 136, 140 and 149)
- Sewing seams (p. 154)

BEFORE YOU BEGIN

Use the long tail cast on method throughout. This cast on produces the equivalent of a row of knit stitches on the needle, so in this stockinette stitch pattern the cast on is counted as the first (RS) row of knitting. If you prefer to use another cast on method, knit one row before continuing with the pattern instructions to keep your row count correct.

The front and back of the kittens are worked from the bottom up.

The color work on the Popcorn and Burger Kittens can be worked using Fair Isle or intarsia techniques.

POPCORN KITTEN

YARN REQUIREMENTS

100g balls (322yd/295m) of Stylecraft Special DK, one in each of Cream 1005 (A), Lipstick 1246 (B), and Citron 1263 (C), or similar yarn (light worsted 100% acrylic)

{01} Make the front and back (both alike)

Using A, cast on 6 sts.

Row 2 and all WS rows (unless stated otherwise): Purl.

Row 3: [Kfb] to end. (12 sts)

Row 5: [Kfb, k1] to end. (18 sts)

Row 7: [Kfb, k2] to end. (24 sts)

Row 9: [Kfb, k3] to end. (30 sts)

Row 11: [Kfb, k4] to end. (36 sts)

Row 13: [Kfb, k5] to end. (42 sts)

Using the Fair Isle or intarsia technique, continue as folls:

Row 15: K4A, [k1B, k5A] 6 times, k1B, k1A.

Row 16: [P3B, p3A] to end.

Row 17: [K3A, k3B] to end.

Row 18: [P3B, p3A] to end.

Repeat rows 17–18 eleven more times.

Row 41: K1C, [k1A, k2C, k1B, k2C] 6 times, k1A, k2C, k1B, k1C. Continue in C only.

Row 42: Purl.

Row 43: [K2tog, k5] to end. (36 sts)

Rows 44–50: Work st st.

Row 51: [K2tog, k4] to end. (30 sts)

Rows 52–58: Work st st.

Row 59: [K2tog, k3] to end. (24 sts)

Work ears as folls:

Row 61: K8 and place onto stitch holder to be worked later, bind off 8 sts, knit to end.

Row 62: Purl the 8 live sts.

Row 63: Skpo, k6. (7 sts)

Row 65: Skpo, k5. (6 sts)

Row 67: Skpo, k2, k2tog. (4 sts)

Bind off.

Place 8 sts from stitch holder onto LH needle with WS facing and rejoin yarn.

Row 62: Purl.

Row 63: K6, k2tog. (7 sts)

Row 65: K5, k2tog. (6 sts)

Row 67: Skpo, k2, k2tog. (4 sts)

Bind off.

{02} Make the tail

Using C, cast on 12 sts.

Row 2 (WS): Purl.

Rows 3–26: Work st st.

Row 27: [K2tog, k1] to end. (8 sts)

Row 28: Purl.

Row 29: [K2tog] to end. (4 sts)

Cut yarn, thread through remaining sts and pull tight.

{03} Add the face

Position the eyes on the front of the kitten, ¾in (2cm) down from the center bound off edge and 1½in (4cm) in from the side edges. Secure with washers. Cut a small triangle of black felt for the nose and four strips for the whiskers. Position the nose in the center of the face, 2 rows down from the eyes. Sew or glue in place. Position the top pair of whiskers in line with the nose, 2 sts to either side of it. Place the bottom pair of whiskers 1 row below the top whiskers, on a slight diagonal. Sew or glue in place.

{04} Make up the kitten

Use mattress stitch and matching yarn to sew up all the pieces. Stitch the front and back pieces together all around the edges, leaving a small gap for stuffing. Lightly stuff, being careful to shape the kitten as desired and not to overstuff; don't stuff the ears. Sew up the gap and weave in the ends.

Fold the tail in half lengthways and sew up, leaving the cast on edge open. Position the open end of the tail centrally underneath the kitten, by the seam, and sew in place. Wrap the tail around to the kitten's front.

Knitting Story

For a while now I have been in love with Japanese kawaii culture. I have always had a secret geeky side, watching anime while knitting away in a Totoro onesie and matching slippers. I had been dreaming of the day I could make these kittens, and when it came I chose the brightest and cutest yarns. I used felt for the whiskers and black toy eyes to create their adorable expressions. I recommend playing around until you find the perfect expression for your kitten. **Louise Walker**

BURGER KITTEN

YARN REQUIREMENTS
100g balls (322yd/295m) of
Stylecraft Special DK, one in each of
Camel 1420 (A), Meadow 1065 (B),
Lipstick 1246 (C), Walnut 1054 (D),
and Citron 1263 (E), or similar yarn
(light worsted 100% acrylic)

{01} Make the front and back (both alike)
Using A, cast on 6 sts and work to
end of row 13 as for popcorn kitten.
Work 9 rows st st.
Using the Fair Isle or intarsia
technique, continue as folls:

Row 23: K3A, k6B, k8A, k4B, k7A, k4B,
k5A, k5B.
Work 5 rows st st in C.
Row 29: K4B, k3C, k5B, k4C, k8B,
k3C, k5B, k3C, k4B, k3A.
Row 30: P11C, p3B, p6C, p4B, p7C,
p3B, p6C, p2B.
Work 4 rows st st in C.
Row 35: K20C, k22D.
Row 36: P34D, p8C.
Work 6 rows st st in D.
Row 43: [K2togD, k5D] to
end. (36 sts)
Row 44: P23D, p7E, p6D.
Rows 45: K2D, k34E.
Work 3 rows st st in E.

Row 49: K24E, k12A.
Row 50: P25A, p11E.
Continue in A only and work as for
popcorn kitten from row 51 to end.

{02} Make up the kitten
Make the tail using A, add the face
and sew up and stuff as instructed
for the popcorn kitten.

LOUISE WALKER

Louise is a knitting pattern author and
commercial photography graduate
living in Brixton, London. Her work
combines her love of humor and
cuteness, and often features animal-
friendly trophy heads. Her debut
book *Faux Taxidermy Knits* includes a
whole horde of wild creatures that she
designed, made, and shot herself—the
photographs, of course! Visit her at
sincerelylouise.blogspot.co.uk

ICE CREAM KITTEN

YARN REQUIREMENTS

200g ball (645yd/590m) of Stylecraft Baby DK in Fondant Marl 1255 (A), or similar yarn (light worsted 100% acrylic)

100g balls (322yd/295m) of Stylecraft Special DK, one in each of Cream 1005 (B), Lipstick 1246 (C), and Black 1002 (D), or similar yarn (light worsted 100% acrylic)

{01} Make the front and back (both alike)
Using A, cast on 6 sts and work to end of row 13 as for popcorn kitten.
Work 29 rows st st.
Work as for popcorn kitten from row 43 to end.

{02} Make the ice cream
Using B, cast on 6 sts.
Row 2 and all WS rows (unless stated otherwise): Purl.
Row 3: [Kfb] to end. (12 sts)
Row 5: [Kfb, k1] to end. (18 sts)
Row 7: [Kfb, k2] to end. (24 sts)
Row 9: [Kfb, k3] to end. (30 sts)
Row 11: [Kfb, k4] to end. (36 sts)
Row 12: [K2, p2] to end.
Repeat row 12 six times more.
Row 19: [K2tog, p2tog] to end. (18 sts)
Row 20: [K1, p1] to end.
Row 21: [K2tog] to end. (9 sts)
Change to C.

Row 23: [Kfb] to end. (18 sts)
Rows 24–28: Work st st.
Row 29: [K2tog] to end. (9 sts)
Change to D.
Row 31: [K2tog, k1] to end. (6 sts)
Work 13 rows st st.
Bind off.

{03} Make up the kitten
Make the tail using A, add the face and sew up and stuff as instructed for the popcorn kitten.
Fold the ice cream in half vertically, aligning the colors, and sew up from the cast on edge to the cherry. Add a small amount of stuffing and finish sewing up. Place the ice cream on top of the kitten's head and sew in place using B.

Lacy top socks

Dip your toes into the wonderful world of sock knitting with this pretty pair. Worked on a circular needle using the magic loop method, they are a great way to learn about how socks are shaped and will prepare you for making more complicated pairs in the future. The lace stitch is a simple eyelet pattern and the yarn is an easy-wear soft wool mix.

MATERIALS

Two 50g balls (136yd/125m) of Debbie Bliss Baby Cashmerino in Duck Egg 26, or similar yarn (light worsted 55% wool, 33% acrylic, 12% cashmere)

32in (80cm) long size 1/2 (2.5mm) circular needle

Three round markers (or use scraps of yarn)

Tapestry needle

SIZE

To fit shoe sizes 7–9 (Euro 38–40/UK 5–7), but size is adjustable

GAUGE

28 sts and 41 rows to 4in (10cm) over st st using size 1/2 needles.

FEATURED TECHNIQUES

- Basic stitch patterns (p. 104)
- Slip stitch edge (p. 108)
- Increasing one knitwise (p. 116)
- Knit two stitches together (p. 118)
- Purl two stitches together (p. 119)
- Pick up and knit (p. 123)
- Short-row shaping (p. 124)
- Lace knitting (p. 129)
- Magic loop technique (p. 134)
- Sewing seams (p. 154)

BEFORE YOU BEGIN

The socks are knitted from the top down and can be altered to fit. A circular needle is used throughout, but you start by working in the round using the magic loop technique for the leg section, then work back and forth in rows for the heel flap and heel turn, and finally revert to circular knitting to complete the socks.

The lace is a simple eyelet pattern worked by repeating a yarnover and decrease across the row to create a regular series of lace holes. Alternate rows are worked in purl stitch.

The heel flap is worked with a slip stitch edge, which makes it easier to pick up stitches precisely and neatly for working the gusset.

{01} Start the socks (make 2)

Cast on 54 sts and divide them evenly onto the two needle tips. Using the magic loop technique, join for working in the round, taking care not to twist sts. Place marker for start of round.

{02} Work the rib edging, lace panel and leg section

Round 1: [K1, p1] to end.
This round forms single rib. Repeat three times more.
Round 5: [P2tog, p12, p2tog, p11] twice. (50 sts)
Round 6: [Yfwd, skpo] to end.
Round 7: Purl.
Rounds 6–7 form lace pattern. Repeat nine times more.
Round 26: [Kfb, k12, kfb, k11] twice. (54 sts)

Round 27: Knit.
Continue in st st (knit every round) until leg measures 6in (15cm) or desired length.

{03} Work the heel flap

Next round: K27 for top of sock (instep), k27 for heel. Turn and work in rows on 27 heel sts only as folls:
Row 1 (WS): Sl1 pwise, p26.
Row 2: Sl1 kwise, knit to end.
Repeat rows 1–2 twelve times more, then row 1 once again.

{04} Work the heel turn

Row 28 (RS): Sl1 kwise, k15, skpo, k1, turn.
Row 29: Sl1 pwise, p6, p2tog, p1, turn.
Row 30: Sl1 kwise, k7, skpo, k1, turn.
Row 31: Sl1 pwise, p8, p2tog, p1, turn.

Row 32: Sl1 kwise, k9, skpo, k1, turn.
Row 33: Sl1 pwise, p10, p2tog, p1, turn.
Row 34: Sl1 kwise, k11, skpo, k1, turn.
Row 35: Sl1 pwise, p12, p2tog, p1, turn.
Row 36: Sl1 kwise, k13, skpo, k1, turn.
Row 37: Sl1 pwise, p14, p2tog, p1, turn. (17 sts rem for heel)

{05} Work the gusset and foot

Next row: Sl1 kwise, k16 heel sts, pick up and knit 15 sts up side of heel flap by knitting into larger slipped sts along side of heel, pm, pick up and knit 1 st in gap between heel and rest of the sock, k27 sts across top of sock, pick up and knit 1 st in gap between sock and heel flap, pm, pick up and knit 15 sts down other side of heel flap. (76 sts)
Knit to 1 st before first marker, place new marker to indicate new start of round and continue shaping foot in rounds using magic loop technique as folls:
Round 1: K1, sm, skpo, knit to 2 sts before next marker, k2tog, sm, knit to end. (74 sts)
Round 2: K1, sm, knit to next marker, sm, knit to end.
Repeat rounds 1–2 until 54 sts remain.
Continue in st st by knitting every round until foot measures 5in (13cm) along side from edge of heel (sock measures 11in/28cm along top of foot from cast on). You can adjust

the length of the foot at this point. The sock foot should be 1¼in (3cm) shorter than your actual foot. Try your sock on to check with the sts still on the circular needle.

{06} Shape the toe and finish off

Next round: K1, k2tog, k21, skpo, k2, k2tog, k21, skpo, k1. (50 sts)
Next round: Knit.
Repeat last 2 rounds three times more, then first round only six times more. (14 sts)
Bind off.
Turn the sock inside out and oversew the toe together to create a flat seam running straight across the end of the foot. Weave in the ends.

Knitting Story

These socks are a good introduction to circular knitting, which is a useful way to work. The magic loop method allows the stitches to be separated by the cord of the circular needle to work on one section at a time, and a marker indicates the beginning of each round. This method means that there is only one small seam at the toe. **Sian Brown**

Fair Isle hot water bottle cover

This brightly colored hot water bottle cover is far too gorgeous to be tucked away under the bed sheets. Indulge yourself in a spot of color work and get to grips with the Fair Isle basics. Don't be intimidated—Fair Isle is just a fancy stripe, after all!

MATERIALS

50g balls (142yd/130m) of Rowan Pure Wool DK, one in each of Kiss 036 (A), Indigo 010 (B), Avocado 019 (D), Ultra 055 (E), Enamel 013 (F), and Hyacinth 026 (G), or similar yarn (light worsted 100% wool)

50g ball (131yd/120m) of Patons Diploma Gold DK in Bright Aqua 6243 (C), or similar yarn (light worsted 55% wool, 25% acrylic, 20% nylon)

Pair of size 3 (3.25mm) and size 6 (4mm) knitting needles

Tapestry needle

Three red buttons, ½in (14mm) in diameter

SIZE

8in (20cm) wide x 11½in (29cm) high to cuff to fit average hot water bottle

GAUGE

25 sts and 30 rows to 4in (10cm) over patt using size 6 needles.

FEATURED TECHNIQUES

- Working from a chart (p. 9)
- Binding off in pattern (p. 113)
- Make one (p. 115)
- Decreasing (pp. 118, 119, 121 and 122)
- Pick up and knit (p. 123)
- Yarn round needle (p. 130)
- Fair Isle (p. 140)
- Sewing seams (p. 154)

BEFORE YOU BEGIN

On the Fair Isle panel, the zigzag and diamond bands at the top and the bottom have 3 sts at the most between colors, so you can simply float the yarns across the back of the fabric without having to catch them in on these parts of the design.

DESIGNED BY CAROL MELDRUM

{01} Make the front panel

Using size 6 needles and A, cast on 35 sts.

Row 1 (WS): Purl.

Row 2: K1, M1, knit to last st, M1, k1. (37 sts)

Row 3: P1, M1, purl to last st, M1, p1. (39 sts)

Repeat rows 2–3 three times more. (51 sts)

Row 10: Knit.

Using the Fair Isle technique and beg with a purl row, work next 61 rows in st st from chart as folls:

RS rows: Work across first 19 sts, then repeat last 16 sts to end.

WS rows: Work across first 16 sts three times, then the last 3 sts.

Continue in A only.

Work 5 rows st st.

Next row (WS): P1, p2tog, purl to last 3 sts, p2tog tbl, p1. (49 sts)

Next row: K1, k2tog tbl, knit to last 3 sts, k2tog, k1. (47 sts)

Work a further 3 rows decreasing as above. (41 sts)

Bind off 3 sts at beg of next 6 rows. (23 sts)

Bind off.

{02} Make the lower back panel

Work as given for front panel until 41 rows of chart have been worked.

Change to size 3 needles and B and continue as folls:

Next row (RS): K3, [p3, k3] to end.

Next row: P3, [k3, p3] to end.

These 2 rows form triple rib. Repeat three times more.

Bind off in rib.

{03} Make the upper back panel

Using size 3 needles and G, cast on 51 sts.

Row 1 (RS): K3, [p3, k3] to end.

Row 2: P3, [k3, p3] to end.

These 2 rows form triple rib.

Row 3: As row 1.

Row 4 (buttonhole row): P3, k3, [p2tog, yrn, p1, rib 15] twice, p2tog, yrn, p1, k3, p3.

Repeat rows 1–2 twice more.

Change to size 6 needles.

Work 2 rows st st.

Work as given for front panel from row 50 of chart to end of front panel.

{04} Make the top cuff

With RS facing, using size 3 needles and A, pick up and knit 23 sts from bound off edge of front panel, then 23 sts from bound off edge of upper back panel. (46 sts)

Row 1 (WS): P2, [k2, p2] to end.

Row 2: K2, [p2, k2] to end.

These 2 rows form double rib. Repeat until work measures 3¼in (8cm) from pick up.

Change to size 6 needles and continue in rib for a further 3¼in (8cm), ending with a WS row.

Bind off in rib.

{05} Make up the cover

Weave in the ends. Pin front and back panels together so that upper back panel overlaps lower back panel on RS of work. Using A and mattress stitch, sew around the outer edges.

Sew up side of top cuff, reversing the top half of the seam so that it can be turned over without the seam showing.

Sew three buttons to the lower back panel rib to match up with the buttonholes.

FAIR ISLE HOT WATER BOTTLE COVER

Yarn Key

- A
- B
- C
- D
- E
- F
- G

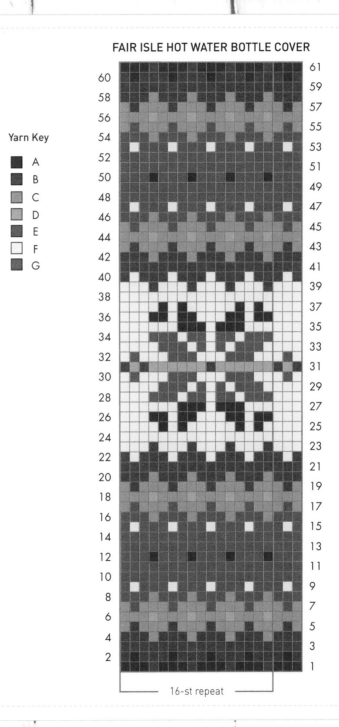

16-st repeat

Bulldog puppy

Out at work all day? You can safely leave Cedric the bulldog to keep a watchful eye over your stuff until your return. Knitted in two parts, his front piece includes the making of his face and a few extra rows for his chin! Horizontal welts are used to create his distinctive wrinkles. Add a fold to his ear and sew on those big button eyes to bring this canine character to life.

MATERIALS

50g balls (126yd/115m) of Todds Hand Knits Zegna Baruffa DK, three in Milk White 301 (A) and one in each of Bordeaux Red 310 (B), Black 330 (C), and Mink Brown 303 (D), or similar yarn (light worsted 100% wool)

Pair of size 6 (4mm) knitting needles

Five stitch markers

Two stitch holders

Tapestry needle

Black toy safety eyes, ¾in (21mm) in diameter, with washers

Black toy nose with washer

Polyester toy stuffing

SIZE

7in (18cm) at widest point x 13¾in (35cm) high to top of head when seated

GAUGE

22 sts and 30 rows to 4in (10cm) over st st using size 6 needles.

FEATURED TECHNIQUES

- Long tail cast on (p. 99)
- Increasing one knitwise (p. 116)
- Decreasing (pp. 118, 119 and 120)
- Welts (p. 126)
- Intarsia (p. 149)
- Sewing seams (p. 154)

BEFORE YOU BEGIN

Use the long tail cast on method throughout. This cast on produces the equivalent of a row of knit stitches on the needle, so in this stockinette stitch pattern the cast on is counted as the first (RS) row of knitting. If you prefer to use another cast on method, knit one row before continuing with the pattern instructions to keep your row count correct.

The front and back of the puppy are worked from the head downward using the intarsia technique.

Welts are worked (on WS rows) above the eyes and nose and on the back to simulate folds of skin.

The cleft in the puppy's chin is formed by creating a hole in the middle of the knitted fabric. The chin is then folded and sewn into place to create the jowls.

Knitting Story

This design was first made when a friend asked for a bulldog as a gift. This happened not long after I first started designing, and so it became an exciting project for me. My friend sent me photographs of her dog, Cedric, and I began researching how I could give my knitting the impression of wrinkles. I love learning new things, especially when they add so much character to a piece, and the horizontal welts were perfect for this pup. *Louise Walker*

{01} Make the front

Using A, cast on 6 sts.

Row 2 and all WS rows (unless stated otherwise): Purl.

Row 3: [Kfb] to end. (12 sts)

Row 5: [Kfb, k1] to end. (18 sts)

Row 7: [Kfb, k2] to end. (24 sts)

Row 9: [Kfb, k3] to end. (30 sts)

Row 11: [Kfb, k4] to end. (36 sts)

Row 13: Knit.

Using the intarsia technique, work eye patches as folls:

Row 15: K6A, k3B, k19A, k3B, k5A.

Row 16: P4A, p5B, p16A, p6B, k5A.

Row 17: K4A, k9B, k13A, k7B, k3A.

Row 18: P3A, p8B, p12A, p9B, p4A.

Row 19: K3A, k11B, k10A, k9B, k3A.

Row 20: P3A, p10B, p9A, p11B, p3A.

Row 21: K3A, k11B, k8A, k11B, k3A.

Row 22: P3A, p11B, p8A, p11B, p3A.

Row 23: As row 21.

Row 24: As row 22.

Row 25: As row 21.

Row 26 (welt row): P3A, *[using RH needle pick up a stitch 6 rows directly below next stitch on LH needle, slip picked up stitch onto LH needle and p2togB] 11 times,* p8A; rep from * to * once more, p3A.

Row 27: K3A, k11B, k8A, k11B, k3A.

Row 28: P3A, p11B, p8A, p11B, p3A.

Row 29: K3A, k9B, k11A, k7B, k6A.

Row 30: P24A, p9B, p3A.

Row 31: K4A, k8B, k24A placing markers on first and 11th of these 24 sts to indicate the position of the eyes.

Start working nose:

Rows 32–41: Work st st in A.

Row 42 (welt row): P6A, [using RH needle pick up a stitch 6 rows directly below next stitch on LH needle, slip picked up stitch onto LH needle and p2togA] 24 times, p6A.

Row 43: K8A, skpoA, k1A, skpoA, k1A, skpoA, k4C, k2togA, k1A, k2togA, k1A, k2togA, k8A. (30 sts)

Row 44: P11A, p8C, p11A.

Row 45: K7A, [skpoA] twice, k8C placing marker on 4th of these 8 sts to indicate position of nose, [k2togA] twice, k7A. (26 sts)

Row 46: P7A, p12C, p7A.

Row 47: K1A, kfbA, k6A, k4D, k2C, k4D, k6A, kfbA, k1A. (28 sts)

Row 48: P9A, p4D, p2C, p4D, p9A.

Row 49: K1A, kfbA, k8A, k3D, k2C, k3D, k8A, kfbA, k1A. (30 sts)

Row 50: P11A, p3D, p2C, p3D, p11A.

Row 51: K1A, kfbA, k11A, k4C, k11A, kfbA, k1A. (32 sts)

Row 52: P12A, p2C, p4D, p2C, p12A.

Row 53: K1A, kfbA, k8A, k3C, k6D, k3C, k8A, kfbA, k1A. (34 sts)

Row 54: P9A, p3C, p3A, p4D, p3A, p3C, p9A.

Row 55: K16A, k2D, k16A.

Continue in A only.

Rows 56–58: Work st st.

Divide for chin cleft:

Row 59: K17, turn and place 17 unworked sts onto a stitch holder.

Row 60: P2tog, p15. (16 sts)

Row 61: Knit.

Row 62: [P2tog] twice, p12. (14 sts)

Row 63: Knit.

Row 65: K12, [kfb] twice. (16 sts)

Row 67: K15, kfb. (17 sts)

Place these 17 sts onto another stitch holder and cut yarn.

Place 17 sts from first stitch holder onto LH needle with RS facing and rejoin yarn.

Row 59: K2tog, k15. (16 sts)

Row 61: [K2tog] twice, k12. (14 sts)

Row 63: Knit.

Row 65: [Kfb] twice, k12. (16 sts)

Row 67: Kfb, k15. (17 sts)

Row 68: P17, place 17 sts from second stitch holder onto LH needle with WS facing and purl to end. (34 sts)

Row 69: Knit.

Row 71: Knit.

Row 73: K1, skpo, k28, k2tog, k1. (32 sts)
Row 75: K1, skpo, k26, k2tog, k1. (30 sts)
Row 77: K1, skpo, k24, k2tog, k1. (28 sts)
Row 78 (ridge row): Knit.
Row 79 (ridge row): Purl.
Row 81: K1, kfb, k24, kfb, k1. (30 sts)

Shape body as folls:
Row 83: K1, kfb, k26, kfb, k1. (32 sts)
Row 85: K1, kfb, k28, kfb, k1. (34 sts)
Row 87: K1, kfb, k30, kfb, k1. (36 sts)
Rows 88–110: Work st st.
Row 111: [Kfb, k5] to end. (42 sts)
Rows 112–126: Work st st.
Row 127: [Kfb, k6] to end. (48 sts)
Rows 128–146: Work st st, placing marker at each end of row 139 for positioning the back legs when making up.
Row 147: [K2tog, k6] to end. (42 sts)
Row 149: [K2tog, k5] to end. (36 sts)
Row 151: [K2tog, k4] to end. (30 sts)
Row 153: [K2tog, k3] to end. (24 sts)
Row 155: [K2tog, k2] to end. (18 sts)
Row 157: [K2tog, k1] to end. (12 sts)
Row 159: [K2tog] to end. (6 sts)
Bind off.

{02} Make the back
Using A, cast on 6 sts.
Row 2 and all WS rows (unless stated otherwise): Purl.
Row 3: [Kfb] to end. (12 sts)
Row 5: [Kfb, k1] to end. (18 sts)
Row 7: [Kfb, k2] to end. (24 sts)

Row 9: [Kfb, k3] to end. (30 sts)
Row 11: [Kfb, k4] to end. (36 sts)
Rows 12–26: Work st st.

Using the intarsia technique, continue as folls:
Row 27: K24A, k5B, k7A.
Row 28: P6A, p7B, p23A.
Row 29: K21A, k10B, k5A.
Row 30: P4A, p14B, p18A.
Row 31: K17A, k17B, k2A.
Row 32: P2A, p19B, p15A.
Row 33: K13A, k21B, k2A.
Row 34: P2A, p23B, p11A.
Row 35: K10A, k24B, k2A.
Row 36: P2A, p25B, p9A.
Row 37: K8A, k26B, k2A.
Row 38: P2A, p27B, p7A.
Row 39: K6A, k28B, k2A.
Row 40: P2A, p28B, p6A.
Row 41: KfbA, k5A, [kfbB, k5B] 4 times, kfbB, k3B, k2A. (42 sts)
Row 42: P2A, p33B, p7A.
Row 43: K7A, k33B, k2A.
Row 44: P2A, p33B, p7A.
Repeat last 2 rows five times more.
Row 55: K9A, k31B, k2A.
Row 56: P2A, p29B, k11A.
Row 57: K13A, k27B, k2A.
Row 58: P2A, p25B, p15A.
Row 59: K16A, k24B, k2A.
Row 60: P2A, p24B, p16A.
Row 61: K16A, k24B, k2A.
Row 62: P2A, p24B, p16A.
Row 63: As row 61.
Row 64: As row 60.
Row 65: K15A, k25B, k2A.
Row 66: P2A, p27B, k13A.

Row 67: K11A, k29B, k2A.
Row 68: P2A, p31B, p9A.
Row 69: K7A, k33B, k2A.
Row 70: P2A, p35B, p5A.
Row 71: K3A, k37B, k2A.
Row 72: P2A, p38B, p2A.
Row 73: K2A, k38B, k2A.
Row 74: P2A, p38B, p2A.
Row 75: As row 73.
Row 76: As row 74.
Row 77: As row 73.

Work folds of skin:
Row 78 (welt row): P2A, p8B, [using RH needle pick up a stitch 6 rows directly below next stitch on LH needle, slip picked up stitch onto LH needle and p2togB] 22 times, p8B, p2A.
Row 79: K2A, k38B, k2A.
Row 80: P2A, p38B, p2A.
Repeat last 2 rows six times more.
Row 93: K2A, k38B, k2A.
Row 94 (welt row): P2A, p6B, [using RH needle pick up a stitch 6 rows directly below next stitch on LH needle, slip picked up stitch onto LH needle and p2togB] 26 times, p6B, p2A.
Row 95: K2A, k37B, k3A.
Row 96: P5A, p35B, p2A.
Row 97: KfbA, k1A, k5B, [kfbB, k6B] 4 times, kfbB, k2B, k4A. (48 sts)
Row 98: P7A, p38B, p3A.
Row 99: K3A, k36B, k9A.
Row 100: P11A, p34B, p3A.
Row 101: K3A, k34B, k11A.
Row 102: P11A, p34B, p3A.

Row 103: K3A, k34B, k11A.
Row 104 (welt row): P11A, p1B, [using RH needle pick up a stitch 6 rows directly below next stitch on LH needle, slip picked up stitch onto LH needle and p2togB] 24 times, p9B, p3A.

Complete back as folls:
Row 105: K3A, k34B, k11A.
Row 106: P11A, p34B, p3A.
Repeat last 2 rows twice more.
Row 111: KfbA, k2A, k5B, [kfbB, k7B] 3 times, kfbB, k4B, k3A, kfbA, k7A. (54 sts)
Row 112: P12A, p36B, p6A.
Row 113: K7A, k13B, k3A, k19B, k12A.
Row 114: P12A, p18B, p5A, p12B, p7A.
Row 115: K9A, k9B, k7A, k17B, k12A.
Row 116: P12A, p17B, p7A, p8B, p10A.
Row 117: K11A, k7B, k7A, k16B, k13A.
Row 118: P13A, p16B, p7A, p7B, p11A.
Row 119: K11A, k6B, k7A, k17B, k13A.
Row 120: P15A, p16B, p6A, p4B, p13A.
Row 121: K13A, k4B, k6A, k14B, k17A.
Row 122: P17A, p14B, p7A, p2B, p14A.
Row 123: K14A, k3B, k8A, k8B, k21A.
Row 124: P23A, p4B, p27A.
Continue in A only.
Row 125: [K2tog, k7] to end. (48 sts)
Row 127: [K2tog, k6] to end. (42 sts)
Row 129: [K2tog, k5] to end. (36 sts)
Row 131: [K2tog, k4] to end. (30 sts)
Row 133: [K2tog, k3] to end. (24 sts)

Row 135: [K2tog, k2] to end. (18 sts)
Row 137: [K2tog, k1] to end. (12 sts)
Row 139: [K2tog] to end. (6 sts)
Bind off.

{03} Make the front legs (make 4)
Using A, cast on 14 sts.
Row 2 (WS): Purl.
Work 28 rows st st.
Row 31: [K2tog] to end. (7 sts)
Bind off.

{04} Make the back legs (make 4)
Using A, cast on 16 sts.
Row 2 (WS): Purl.
Work 42 rows st st.
Row 45: [K2tog, k2] to end. (12 sts)
Row 46: Purl.
Row 47: [K2tog, k1] to end. (8 sts)
Row 48: Purl.
Row 49: [K2tog] to end. (4 sts)
Row 50: Purl.
Bind off.

{05} Make the tail (make 2)
Using A, cast on 10 sts.
Row 2 (WS): Purl.
Work 6 rows st st.
Row 9: Kfb, k8, kfb. (12 sts)
Row 10: Purl.
Work 4 rows st st.
Row 15: [K2tog, k1] to end. (8 sts)
Row 16: Purl.
Row 17: [K2tog] to end. (4 sts)
Row 18: Purl.
Bind off.

{06} Make the ears (make 2 in A and 2 in B)
Cast on 15 sts.
Row 2 (WS): Purl.
Work 14 rows st st.
Row 17: [Skpo] twice, k7, [k2tog] twice. (11 sts)
Row 18: Purl.
Row 19: [Skpo] twice, k3, [k2tog] twice. (7 sts)
Row 20: Purl.
Row 21: Skpo, k3, k2tog. (5 sts)
Row 22: Purl.
Bind off.

{07} Sew up and stuff the pieces
On front of puppy, position eyes and nose at markers on rows 31 and 45 and secure with washers.
The hole in the middle of the front will form the cleft of the puppy's chin. Fold the chin across the middle of the hole (approx along row 63), with WS together and the upper and lower edges of the hole aligned.

Pin the side edges of the chin together as far as the upper ridge row (row 78). Using mattress stitch and A for all seams, sew up the hole and the side edges of the chin. With RS outward, pin back and front together. Sew all around the edges, taking extra care near the puppy's chin and leaving a small gap in the side for stuffing.

Fill with toy stuffing, being careful to shape the puppy and not to overstuff it, and adding a small amount of stuffing to the chin. Neatly sew up the gap and weave in the ends.

Pin and sew two front leg pieces together, leaving the cast on edges open. Fill with stuffing and set aside. Repeat with the second front leg, both back legs, the tail, and both ears, but use B to sew up the colored ear.

{08} Make up the puppy

Using A, pin and sew all four legs to the front of the puppy. Position each front leg 4 rows down from the lower ridge row (row 79) and 5 sts in from the side seams. Position each back leg 3 sts in from side seams at row 139 (marked row).

Position the tail in the center of the back piece, 1 row down from the final color change to yarn A (row 125). Sew into place using A. Position the ears along the seam of the head, with the A ear on the left, the B ear on the right, and 1½in (4cm) between them in the center. Pin and sew in place using matching yarn. Fold over the tip of the B ear and sew into place.

Weave in all ends. If desired, embroider a few lines onto the bottom of the feet using C.

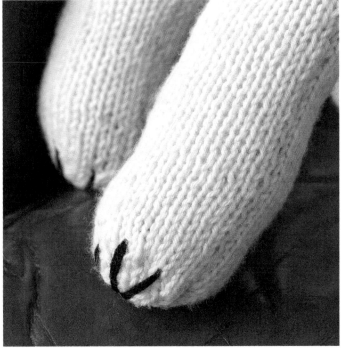

New to knitting?

This section of the book contains all the step-by-step guidance you need to get started. So grab your needles, choose your yarn, and read on—you'll soon discover that there isn't a lot to learn before you can start knitting.

Seasoned pro?

If you've already completed a few knitting projects, use this section to build up your skill base. Packed with hints, tips, and techniques, you'll soon be tackling more complex shaping and stitch patterns with confidence. Have a go at cables, bobbles, loops, and lace, then try your hand at circular knitting and multicolored designs.

Techniques

Needles and yarns

{ *Knitting always begins with a pair of needles and some yarn. Knitting needles come in different thicknesses, referred to as the needle size, and the size you use will depend on the thickness of your yarn. This section has all the information you need to buy needles and yarns with confidence, as well as other useful items.*

NEEDLES

There are three basic types of needle—straight, double-pointed, and circular—available in a range of sizes and lengths, and made from a variety of materials.

STRAIGHT NEEDLES

These are used in pairs. They have a point at one end and a fixed stopper at the other end. Stitches are worked using the pointed end and cannot be removed from the fixed stopper end. Straight needles are used for flat knitting, working across a row of stitches moving them from one needle to the other, turning the work, and working back again.

DOUBLE-POINTED NEEDLES

These are used in sets of four or five needles and have a point at both ends, and this means that stitches can be worked with one end and can also be removed from the other end, avoiding the need to turn your work at the end of each row. These needles are used for working in a round (circular knitting), to make socks for example. Always keep sets of double-pointed needles tied together with an elastic band as it is very easy to lose one.

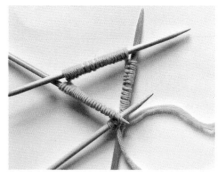

A set of four double-pointed needles being used for working in the round (p. 135).

CIRCULAR NEEDLE

This is a knitting needle with two pointed metal or wooden ends joined by a flexible cord that is usually made of plastic or nylon. As with double-pointed needles you can work from both ends, to knit in rounds to produce a seamless tube (circular knitting). Circular needles come in different lengths to suit the size of the project you are making. You can also work backward and forward on circular needles, which is useful for very large projects such as blankets.

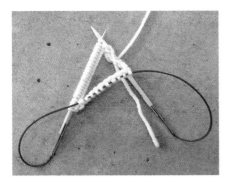

A circular needle being used for working in the round using the magic loop technique (p. 134).

NEEDLE SIZES

The size of a needle is determined by its diameter (thickness). There are three systems of sizing needles. A metric system is used in Europe and the UK; the US has its own system; and an old UK and Canadian system also exists. The table below gives you the equivalent sizes across all three systems.

Metric	US	Old UK & Canadian	Metric	US	Old UK & Canadian
25mm	50	-	5mm	8	6
19mm	35	-	4.5mm	7	7
15mm	19	-	4mm	6	8
12mm	17	-	3.75mm	5	9
10mm	15	000	3.5mm	4	-
9mm	13	00	3.25mm	3	10
8mm	11	0	3mm	2/3	11
7.5mm	11	1	2.75mm	2	12
7mm	10½	2	2.25mm	1	13
6.5mm	10½	3	2mm	0	14
6mm	10	4	1.75mm	00	-
5.5mm	9	5	1.5mm	000	-

Note

There is a huge choice of knitting needles available in different woods and materials including bamboo, plastic, and metal. Choice is a matter of personal preference, so try out different materials to find the one you most enjoy knitting with. The key to good needles is for them to be flexible, smooth, and have well-shaped points. A word of warning: lovely decorative tops look beautiful but they can make the needles heavy and may give you wrist problems.

OTHER EQUIPMENT

There are some other pieces of equipment that you will need to make the projects in this book. Also listed below are a few things that you may find useful as you build up your knitting skills.

Needle size gauge: A useful piece of equipment to check the size of a needle if unknown. It is a strip of plastic with holes punched out marked up with metric and US/UK equivalencies (see Needle Sizes, p. 89). To find the size of a needle, simply insert it through the holes on the size gauge until you get a snug fit.

Tape measure and ruler: You'll need a tape measure to check the measurements of your knitted fabric and a ruler for measuring your gauge square. Be sure to buy a new tape measure regularly as they can stretch over time.

Scissors: Always cut yarn with a pair of scissors; don't try to break it by pulling as this will stretch the fibers and can hurt your hands.

Point protectors: Usually made from plastic, these can be placed on the pointed end of your needles to stop stitches slipping off when not in use; they also prevent needles punching holes in your knitting bag.

Row counter: This slides on to the needle and is turned after each row is completed to help you keep track of the number of rows that have been worked.

Stitch holders: These are used when you need to put a number of stitches to one side while knitting on the remaining stitches, for example, when knitting the ears on the Kawaii Kittens (see p. 66). It is useful to have a variety of sizes of holder as sometimes you need to hold only two or three stitches (a safety pin is ideal in this case) and at other times you need to hold a lot of stitches. A large holder will just get in the way if you are holding only a few stitches. A double-ended holder allows you to knit straight off the holder rather than having to put the stitches onto a knitting needle first.

Markers: Round markers are mostly used when working circular knitting (p. 133). They are slipped onto a needle between stitches to mark the beginning of a round, or increase or decrease points. Stitch markers are looped through a knitted stitch to mark a point in the project that you need to refer back to later, for example, when shaping the Lacy Top Socks (p. 72).

Pins: When blocking (p. 153) and then sewing up (p. 154) a project you will require pins. Long, thick pins with heads are best as they are less likely to split the yarn and are easy to see.

Tapestry needle: Use a blunt-tipped tapestry needle with a large eye for sewing up seams. If you use mattress stitch (p. 154) you will find a sewing needle with a bent tip very useful as it makes it easy to see where it is coming through the knitted stitches.

Cable needles: These are small double-pointed needles used to manipulate stitches when working cables (p. 127). They come in different sizes and styles. Always try to match the size of the cable needle to the size of the knitting needles you are using. A cranked needle (see note on p. 128) is a good choice when you are learning to cable, as it makes it almost impossible to drop a stitch while you are working the cable twist.

Bobbins: These are plastic holders for winding small amounts of yarn onto when intarsia knitting (p. 149).

Note

There is a huge choice of lovely knitting equipment and it can be tempting to buy things that are pretty; just make sure they are practical as well. For example, overly ornate round markers can catch in knitted fabric.

YARN

Yarns are available in a vast range of weights, colors, textures, and fibers. Choosing the correct yarn can make all the difference between success and disappointment when knitting a project.

FIBER CONTENT

The fibers used to spin yarns may be natural, synthetic, or a mixture of the two. The different fibers have varying properties and so the yarns made from them will be suitable for different types of project.

Wool yarns: Wool is a warm fiber that can also breathe. Wool yarns are generally easy to knit with and their elasticity is quite forgiving if your gauge is a little uneven.

Cotton yarns: Cotton is kind on the skin and cool to wear, but is heavier and less elastic than wool. It shows stitch detail well and so is great for knitting textured patterns.

Synthetic yarns: These are usually washable, durable, and cheaper than natural fiber yarns. Novelty yarns are generally made from synthetic fibers.

Mixed fiber yarns: The addition of small amounts of synthetic fiber will make a yarn lighter and more elastic. If you find pure wool too itchy, then try a wool and cotton mix. Silk mix yarns have a soft sheen and a luxurious feel.

Cotton/elastane mix T-shirt yarn.

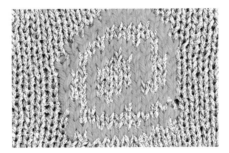
Metallic and wool/synthetic mix yarns.

Alpaca yarn.

YARN WEIGHT

This refers to the thickness of the yarn, not the number of grams in the ball. There are names for standard weights of yarn, such as DK (double knitting) and 4ply (both European terms; see the table overleaf for standard yarn weight conversions). Yarns are made by spinning together a number of strands, or plies, and the general rule is that the lower the number of plies, the finer the yarn. However, thick yarns can in fact be made from just one ply or thin yarns from four plies, and there are lots of yarns that do not fit into the standard weight categories. The ball band of the yarn should include the average gauge (p. 10) and needle size (p. 89) recommended by the manufacturer, and you can use the table overleaf as a guide to identify the weight of a yarn if it is unclear.

SUBSTITUTING A YARN

If you are buying the yarn recommended in a pattern then you just have to choose the color, but if you would prefer to use a different yarn, then it is possible to change it.

The simplest option is to choose a substitute yarn that is the same weight as the pattern yarn. However, yarns of the same weight do not always knit up to the same gauge, so you really must make a gauge square (p. 10). Check the ball band for the average gauge of the substitute yarn, and as long as this doesn't differ by more than one stitch from that of the pattern yarn, you should be able to achieve the right gauge by changing needle size. More than one stitch difference could cause you a lot of problems; it's better to look for a different yarn. If you choose a substitute yarn with a different fiber content, remember that this will affect the appearance, feel, and drape of the knitted fabric.

Even though the balls of substitute yarn may weigh the same as those of the pattern yarn, they may not contain the same number of yards. This is particularly true if you are changing fiber—for example, cotton is heavier than wool so there will be fewer yards to a 50g ball than there will be of wool yarn. To calculate how many balls of substitute yarn to buy, work out the total yardage of the original yarn, then divide this by the yardage of one ball of your chosen alternative.

YARN STANDARDS

The Craft Yarn Council of America has a system of categorizing yarns that you may find useful. It provides a guide only and you should always use the gauge and needle size given in the pattern you are following.

Yarn weight symbol	Yarn category names	Recommended US (metric) needle size	Gauge range in stockinette stitch over 4in (10cm)
0 LACE	4ply, 10-count crochet thread (fingering)	000–1 (1.5–2.25mm)	33–40 sts
1 SUPER FINE	4ply, sock, baby (fingering)	1–3 (2.25–3.25mm)	27–32 sts
2 FINE	Light-weight DK, baby (sport)	3–5 (3.25–3.75mm)	23–26 sts
3 LIGHT	DK (light-weight worsted)	5–7 (3.75–4.5mm)	21–24 sts
4 MEDIUM	Aran (worsted, afghan)	7–9 (4.5–5.5mm)	16–20 sts
5 BULKY	Chunky (craft, rug)	9–11 (5.5–8mm)	12–15 sts
6 SUPER BULKY	Super chunky (bulky, roving)	11–17 (8–12.75mm)	7–11 sts
7 JUMBO	Jumbo	17 and larger (12.75mm and larger)	6 sts and fewer

Source: Craft Yarn Council's
www.YarnStandards.com

HOLDING NEEDLES AND YARN

One of the first steps in learning to knit is to choose which way to hold the needles and yarn. There are several ways of doing this, and you should choose the one that feels most comfortable.

Note

Although awkward at first, you will find that holding the needles becomes much more comfortable with practice. Have a go at each method and you will quickly find out which one is most suitable for you. Once you are able to control the needles, ignore them for a while and learn to knit. You can always return to perfect your holding technique later.

THE ENGLISH METHOD

The needles are held differently in the right and left hands, and the yarn is held in your right hand.

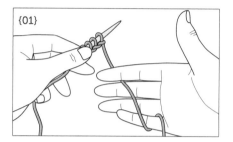

{01}

Hold the needle that carries the stitches in your left hand. Wrap the yarn around the little finger of your right hand and then come up between your index and second fingers.

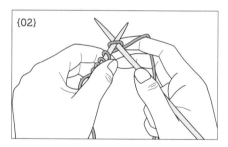

{02}

Hold the other needle in your right hand, placing it in the crook between the thumb and index finger, in the same way as you would hold a pencil. The right-hand index finger is going to control the gauge of the yarn, so it is important to keep the yarn slightly taut around this finger.

THE SCOTTISH METHOD

This way of holding the yarn and needles originated in the north of Britain. Some knitters tuck the end of the right-hand needle under their arm when using this method.

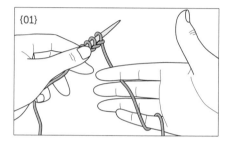

{01}

Hold the needle that carries the stitches in your left hand. Wrap the yarn around the little finger of your right hand and then come up between your index and second fingers.

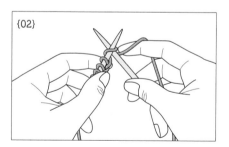

{02}

Hold the other needle in your right hand, placing your hand on top of the needle, in the same way as you would hold a knife. The right-hand index finger is going to control the gauge of the yarn, so it is important to keep the yarn slightly taut around this finger.

THE CONTINENTAL METHOD

For this method, the working yarn is held in your left hand.

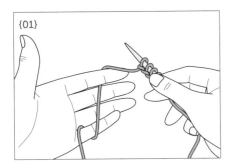

{01}

Hold the needle that carries the stitches in your right hand. Wrap the yarn around the little finger and then around the index finger of your left hand. Then move the needle holding the stitches into your left hand.

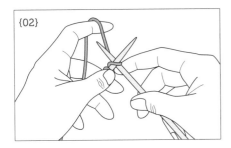

{02}

Hold the other needle in your right hand, holding it from above. The gauge of the yarn will be controlled by your left-hand index finger, so it is important to keep the yarn around it slightly taut.

Knitting basics

{ *Knitting is a series of loops of yarn locked together to make a fabric. The loops are called stitches. They are held on a needle, then more stitches are worked into them with the other needle, at the same time transferring the stitches from one needle to the other. Repeating this process row by row creates the knitted fabric.*

CASTING ON

To start knitting you need to get the required number of loops, or stitches, onto the needle—this is called casting on. There are several ways to cast on stitches, each producing a slightly different edge. Which method you choose is largely down to personal preference, although some methods may be better for starting certain stitches.

Note

There are just two stitches you need to master to be able to do all types of knitting: the knit stitch and the purl stitch. These stitches put together enable you to make a whole range of textures. The methods for working these stitches are explained on pp. 100–103.

The smooth edge of a cable cast on looks good with stockinette stitch.

The long tail cast on edge gives a similar end result to the thumb cast on.

The ridged edge of a thumb cast on will look particularly good with garter stitch and seed stitch.

The Tweed Stitch Rug (p. 28) is bound off on a wrong-side row so that it looks like the thumb cast on at the other end of the rug.

THE SLIP KNOT

To cast on you need a starting point—this is the slip knot. The slip knot will always count as the first cast on stitch.

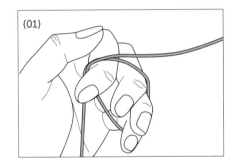

{01}

Hold the working (ball) end of the yarn in your right hand and wrap it around the fingers of your left hand.

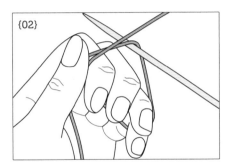

{02}

Put the tip of a knitting needle, held in your right hand, through the loop around your fingers.

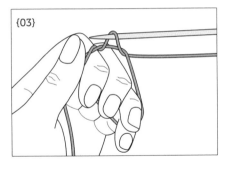

{03}

Wrap the working end of the yarn around the needle and pull the needle, and the yarn wrapped around it, through the loop around your left hand.

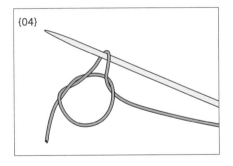

{04}

Keeping the yarn on the needle, slip the loop off your left hand.

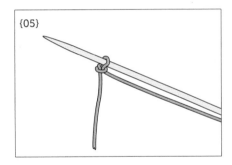

{05}

Pull gently on the ends of the yarn so that the loop tightens around the needle.

Note

Whatever cast on technique you use, do not cast on too tightly. If your stitches do not move freely along the needle, try using a larger needle.

CABLE CAST ON

This technique gives a firm edge that keeps its shape well over time, making it ideal for firm stitches such as stockinette stitch. It is worked using two needles.

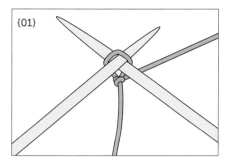

{01}

Make a slip knot about 6in (15cm) from the end of the yarn. Hold the needle with the slip knot in your left hand and the other needle in your right. With the working end of the yarn in your right hand, put the tip of the right-hand needle into the stitch on the left-hand needle.

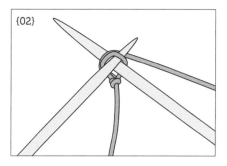

{02}

Bring the yarn in your right hand under and around the point of the right-hand needle. Pull the yarn taut so that it is wrapped around the tip of the right-hand needle.

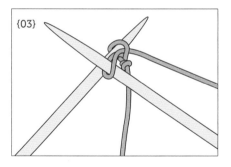

{03}

Bring the tip of the right-hand needle, and the yarn wrapped around it, through the stitch and toward you.

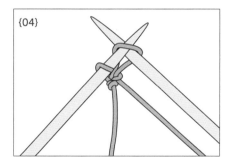

{04}

Pull gently until the loop is large enough to slip it over the tip of the left-hand needle as shown. Take the right-hand needle out of the loop and pull the working end of the yarn so that the loop fits snugly around the left-hand needle.

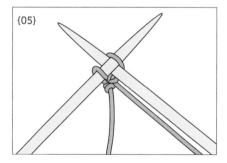

{05}

To cast on all the other stitches, put the tip of the right-hand needle between the last two stitches instead of through the last one. Then repeat steps 2–5 until you have the required number of stitches on the left-hand needle.

Note

If you find it difficult to push the right-hand needle between the stitches in step 5, try putting it through before you tighten the last stitch in step 4. With the needle in place, pull the last stitch tight, then work the next one.

THUMB CAST ON

The thumb technique produces an edge that has elasticity. This is very useful when working with yarns that don't have a lot of give, such as chenille or firm cotton, or when casting on for a ribbed edge. It is also a cast on that looks good with garter stitch and seed stitch.

Note

For this cast on you first need to pull enough yarn from the ball to make all the stitches. Allowing approx. ¾in (2cm) per stitch, measure out the correct amount of yarn, then make a slip knot.

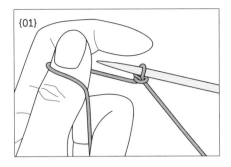

{01}

Hold the ball end of the yarn and the needle in your right hand. Hold the other end of the yarn (the measured length) in the palm of your left hand. Move your left thumb behind and under the yarn, so that the yarn is wrapped from front to back around your left thumb.

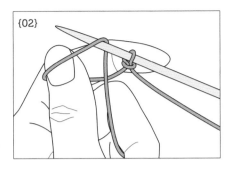

{02}

Insert the tip of the needle into the loop on your thumb.

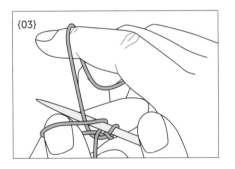

{03}

Wrap the yarn in your right hand under and around the tip of the knitting needle.

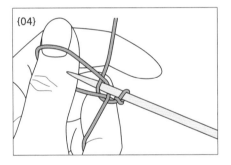

{04}

Bring the needle, and the yarn wrapped around it, through the loop around your thumb and toward you to make another stitch on the needle.

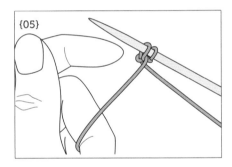

{05}

Slip your thumb out of the loop and pull the two ends of yarn away from the needle in opposite directions. Repeat steps 2–5 until you have cast on the number of stitches required.

LONG TAIL CAST ON

If you hold the needles and knit in the continental style (see p. 94 and pp. 102–103), try this cast on: it gives a similar end result to the thumb cast on. You need to calculate how much yarn you will use allowing ¾in (2cm) per stitch. Measure out the correct amount of yarn, then make a slip knot.

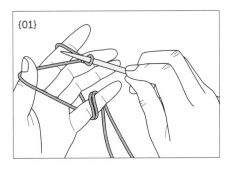

{01}

Wrap the ball end of the yarn around your left index finger and the measured end around your left thumb. Wrap both ends around your little finger to hold them in place.

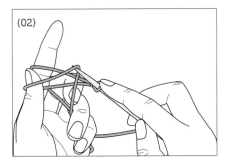

{02}

Holding the needle in your right hand, put the tip of it up through the loop around your thumb.

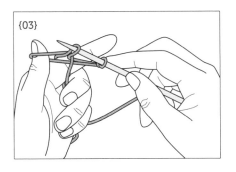

{03}

Now take it down through the loop around your index finger and then back under the loop on your thumb.

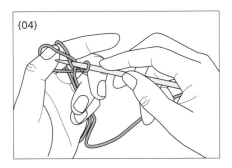

{04}

Slip your thumb out of its loop, making sure you don't drop the loop off the needle.

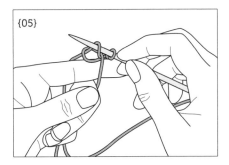

{05}

Using your left thumb, pull the new loop on the needle tight to complete the stitch. Repeat steps 1–5 until you have cast on the number of stitches that are required.

Note

If your stitches are too tight, try casting on onto two needles held together. When you have cast on all the stitches, slip one needle out of them before knitting the first row.

KNIT AND PURL STITCH PATTERN ABBREVIATION: K AND P

Once you have cast on the required number of stitches, you can start to make your knitted fabric. When you knit, you transfer stitches from the left-hand needle to the right-hand needle. When you come to the end of the row, you put the needle with the stitches on into your left hand and work on the reverse side of the project to knit, or purl, the next row. There are two main styles of knitting: English and continental.

Note

You can knit every stitch on every row and this will give you a texture called garter stitch (p. 104). Most knitting designs are made up of both knit and purl stitches. It's best to practice the knit stitch until you are confident with it and then move on to purl stitch.

ENGLISH METHOD: KNIT STITCH

Hold the needles using either the English method or the Scottish method (p. 93).

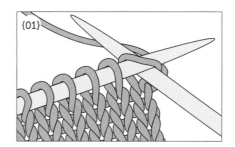

{01}

From front to back, insert the tip of the right-hand needle into the first stitch on the left-hand needle. Bring the yarn you are holding in your right hand under the tip of the right-hand needle.

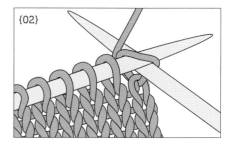

{02}

Wrap the yarn over the needle.

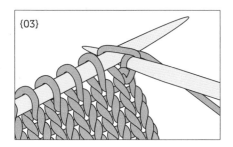

{03}

Bring the tip of the right-hand needle and yarn wrapped around it through the stitch on the left-hand needle.

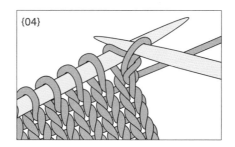

{04}

Pull the loop of yarn through to make a new stitch on the right-hand needle.

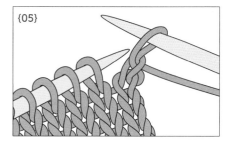

{05}

Slip the original stitch off the left-hand needle. The knit stitch is complete.

ENGLISH METHOD: PURL STITCH

Hold the needles using either the English method or the Scottish method (p. 93).

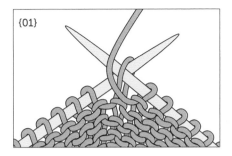

{01}

For purl stitch, you need the yarn at the front of the work as shown. From back to front, put the tip of the right-hand needle into the next stitch on the left-hand needle. Bring the yarn forward and then take it over the tip of the right-hand needle.

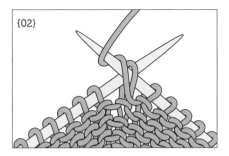

{02}

Wrap the yarn under and around the tip of the needle.

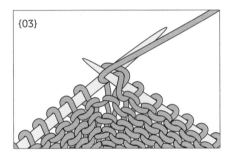

{03}

Bring the tip of the right-hand needle, and the yarn wrapped around it, backward through the stitch on the left-hand needle, making sure that this stitch remains on the needle.

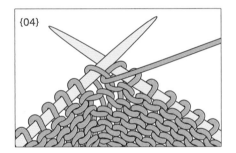

{04}

Pull the loop completely through the stitch, creating a new stitch on the right-hand needle.

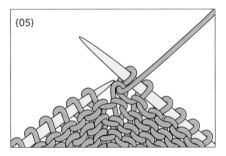

{05}

When it's safely through, slip the original stitch off the left-hand needle. The purl stitch is now complete.

CONTINENTAL METHOD: KNIT STITCH

If you are going to use the continental techniques, this is how you work a knit stitch.

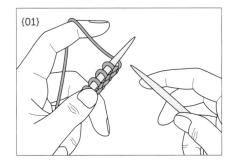

Hold the needles using the continental method (p. 94).

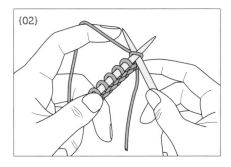

From front to back, put the tip of the right-hand needle into the first stitch on the left-hand needle.

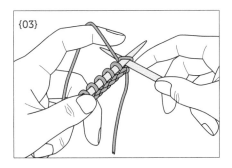

Lay the yarn that is held in your left hand over the right-hand needle, as shown.

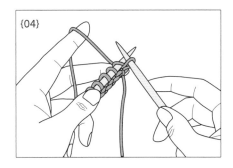

With the tip of the right-hand needle, bring the strand through the cast on stitch. You will need to lower your left-hand index finger slightly to help this process.

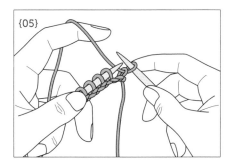

Slip the original stitch off the left-hand needle. The knit stitch is now complete.

CONTINENTAL METHOD: PURL STITCH

This is how you work a purl stitch using the continental technique.

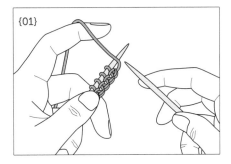

{01}

Bring the yarn to the front of the left-hand needle.

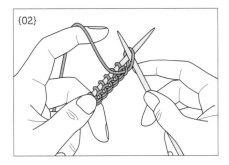

{02}

From back to front, put the tip of the right-hand needle into the first stitch on the left-hand needle.

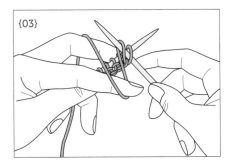

{03}

Lay the yarn over the tip of the right-hand needle and use the index finger of the left hand to keep the yarn taut.

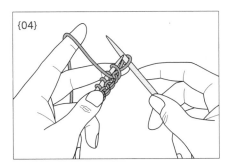

{04}

Move the tip of the right-hand needle backward through the stitch on the left-hand needle, making sure that this stitch remains on the needle.

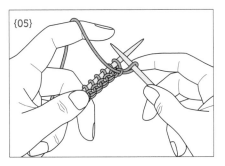

{05}

When it's safely through, slip the original stitch off the left-hand needle. The purl stitch is now complete.

AT THE END OF A ROW

You have learned how to knit a stitch and then how to purl one, but how do you put these together?

The easiest thing to do is to cast on 20 or 30 stitches (use a cable cast on or thumb cast on for the English method, or the long tail cast on for the continental method) and then practice the knit stitch. When you have knitted every stitch from the left-hand needle to the right-hand needle you need to turn the work. Simply swap the needles in your hands so that the needle with the stitches on is now the left-hand needle and the empty needle is now the right-hand one. You are ready to start the next row.

To make a stockinette stitch fabric (the most common knitted fabric), purl the next row. When you have finished purling the row, the yarn will be at the front of the work. Wrap it around to the other side of the work, which will tighten up the last stitch, and then swap the needles in your hands. Continue alternating knit and purl rows for the length of fabric you wish to make.

BASIC STITCH PATTERNS

Once you have learned the knit and purl stitches, a world of knitted fabrics is open to you. Here are the most commonly used and simplest fabrics you will now be able to make.

The Christmas Tree Decorations (p. 12) are made using basic stitch patterns: stockinette stitch for the Santa and elf, and garter stitch for the present.

GARTER STITCH

If you knit every stitch and every row you will make a fabric called garter stitch. This fabric is great for beginners and is perfect for making a scarf as it is completely reversible.

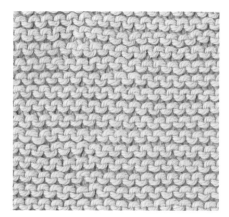

Garter stitch.

STOCKINETTE STITCH (UK STOCKING STITCH)
PATTERN ABBREVIATION: ST ST

The most common knitted fabric is stockinette stitch. It is made by working alternate rows of knit and purl stitches.

This is the right side of stockinette stitch. This is also known as the knit side, as it is the knit stitches that form the interlocked V shapes.

REVERSE STOCKINETTE STITCH (UK REVERSE STOCKING STITCH)
PATTERN ABBREVIATION: REV ST ST

This is quite simply the reverse side of stockinette stitch. This fabric is often used as a background for cables and other textured stitches (pp. 127–128).

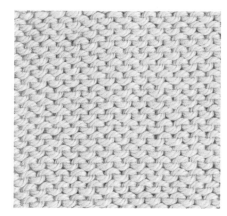

This is the wrong side of stockinette stitch, and forms a stitch in its own right called reverse stockinette stitch. It is known as the purl side, as it is the purl stitches that form the bumps on the fabric.

RIB

If you were to cast on and work in stockinette stitch straight away, the lower edge of your work would curl up. This is sometimes used as a feature, but to eliminate this curl you can use a rib for a neat edge with the knit and purl stitches forming distinctive columns, as on the cuffs and neckbands of garments for example. Rib is very elastic, so it stretches to allow a hand or head to pass through and then closes up again for a snug fit.

The stitches in single rib fabric run in columns.

SINGLE RIB PATTERN ABBREVIATION: K1, P1 RIB

Also known as 1x1 rib, this is formed by alternately knitting one stitch and then purling one stitch.

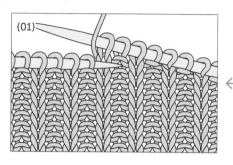

Knit one stitch with the yarn at the back of the work, then bring the yarn forward between the tips of the needles to the front in order to purl one stitch. When you have completed the purl stitch, take the yarn back between the needles ready for the next knit stitch.

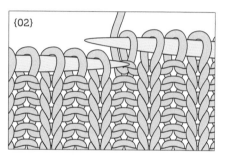

Here the yarn is at the back of the work ready to knit the next stitch.

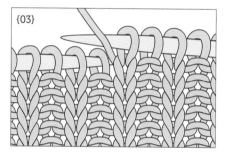

Here the yarn has come between the needles to be at the front ready for the purl stitch.

Note

If you don't take the yarn to the front and back between stitches you will end up with loops lying across the needles. If you have more stitches than you should at the end of a row then this may have occurred.

RIB PATTERNS

Combining various numbers of knit and purl stitches will create different rib patterns. For example, alternating two knit stitches and two purl stitches produces double rib (or 2x2 rib); alternating three knit stitches and three purl stitches produces triple rib (or 3x3 rib). You can alternate different numbers of knit and purl stitches, such as 4x2 rib. Working knit stitches through the back loop (p. 107) twists them, giving the rib pattern a different look.

SEED STITCH (UK MOSS STITCH)

Seed stitch is a knitted stitch pattern that creates a firm, dense fabric made by alternating knit and purl stitches. It is formed by knitting one stitch and purling the next, like rib, but the difference is that on the second row you work the opposite stitch to the one in the previous row. Rather than lining up in columns, the stitches produce a bumpy, textured fabric.

Note

Seed stitch is perfect for accessories such as scarves and bags as it is both stable and reversible. Different combinations of knit and purl stitches will create different seed patterns.

WORKING SEED STITCH

Knit one stitch with the yarn at the back of the work, then bring the yarn forward between the tips of the needles to the front in order to purl one stitch. When you have completed the purl stitch, take the yarn back between the needles ready for the next knit stitch.

On the second row, when you are faced with a knit stitch you purl it; when faced with a purl stitch, you knit it. In the diagram above, a stitch that was purled on the previous row will be knitted on this row.

WHICH STITCH NEXT IN SEED?

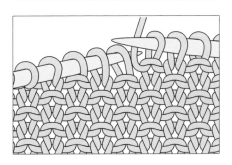

If the next stitch has a bump across the bottom of it, then it is a purl stitch and you must knit into it. Conversely, if the next stitch is smooth then it is a knit stitch and you must purl into it. The next stitch worked in the diagram (right) will be a knit stitch.

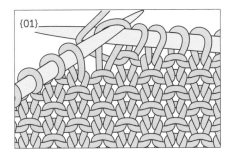

The textured fabric of the Twisted Headband (p. 18) is created using seed stitch.

THROUGH THE BACK LOOP OF A STITCH
PATTERN ABBREVIATION: TBL

When you work a standard knit or purl stitch, you insert the right-hand needle through the front loop of the stitch on the left-hand needle, but the technique explained here involves working through the back loop of the stitch instead. This twists the stitch being worked, giving it a different appearance. In the diagrams, the column of stitches below the one being worked have all been worked through the back loop.

The shaping for the bottom of the Seed Stitch Pot (p. 41) involves knitting through the back loops.

KNITTING THROUGH THE BACK LOOP

Here you are knitting through the back of the stitch, rather than through the front as is usual.

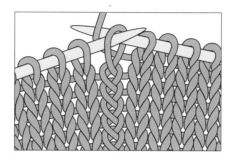

From front to back, put the tip of the right-hand needle into the back loop of the next stitch on the left-hand needle. Wrap the yarn around the tip of the needle and pull the new stitch through in the usual way.

PURLING THROUGH THE BACK LOOP

Although this looks complicated, you are simply purling through the back loop of the stitch.

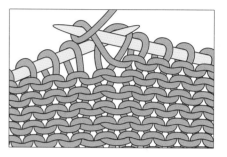

From back to front, put the tip of the right-hand needle into the back loop of the next stitch. Wrap the yarn around the tip of the needle and pull the new stitch through in the usual way.

Note

Purling through the back loops is slightly tricky; a good tip is to put the right-hand needle into the front of the stitch first and give it a slight stretch. Then hold the stitch in place with your left index finger on the left-hand needle while putting the right-hand needle through the stitch to knit it.

SLIPPING STITCHES

When you need to move a stitch from the left-hand needle to the right-hand needle without actually knitting or purling it, then you must slip it. This technique is used in different ways in knitting, such as for working decreases, creating lace patterns, and adding a slip stitch selvedge, and is something you need to learn.

SLIPPING A STITCH KNITWISE
PATTERN ABBREVIATION: SL KWISE

You would usually slip a stitch this way on a knit row, although some effects involve slipping a stitch the opposite way to the stitches that are actually being worked.

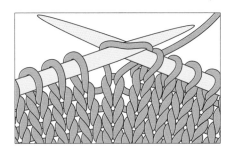

From front to back, put the tip of the right-hand needle into the next stitch on the left-hand needle and slip it over onto the right-hand needle.

SLIPPING A STITCH PURLWISE
PATTERN ABBREVIATION: SL PWISE

This is the method you use to slip a stitch purlwise, on a purl or a knit row.

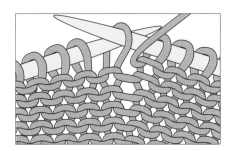

From back to front, put the tip of the right-hand needle into the next stitch on the left-hand needle and slip it over onto the right-hand needle.

SLIP STITCH EDGE

When working a piece of knitting it can become uneven at the edges. You can neaten them by adding a selvedge, which is simply an edge created by working the first and last one or two stitches in a different stitch pattern to the rest of the row. A slip stitch edge, for example, helps to neaten the edges of the Baby Blanket (p. 22). Simply slip the first stitch on every row. Unless specified otherwise, slip the stitch knitwise on knit rows and purlwise on purl rows. However, some pattern designers recommend slipping the first stitch knitwise on both knit and purl rows. If a pattern does not specify, it is worth experimenting with both methods to see which result you prefer.

Note

When you are slipping a stitch be very careful not to pull on it and stretch it as there is nothing going through it to tighten it up again. Put the very tip of the needle into the stitch and allow it to find its own shape on the right-hand needle. A stretched slipped stitch will show in the finished knitting.

JOINING IN A NEW BALL OF YARN

Unless your project is very small, you will at some point finish a ball of yarn and need to join in a new one. You should always join in new yarn at the edge of your work, so when your yarn is running low it is important to check that you have sufficient to get to the other end of a row as described here, and if not, join in a new ball as described.

CALCULATING YARN FOR STOCKINETTE STITCH

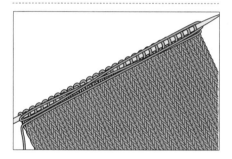

If you are working in stockinette stitch, spread the knitting out flat across the needle. Loop the yarn back and forth across the knitting. If the yarn measures three times the width of your knitting then you have enough to do one more row. If it measures less, then start a new ball. Cut the long end, leaving 6in (15cm) to weave in (p. 152).

Note

If your work is too wide to lie flat on one needle, measure the width and then measure the length of the yarn remaining instead of looping it across the needle.

CALCULATING YARN FOR STITCH PATTERNS

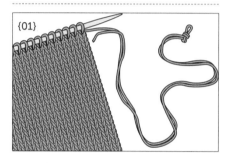

When you are getting near the end of the ball, fold the yarn remaining in half and place a slip knot at the fold.

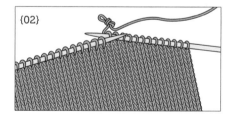

If you come to the slip knot on the next row, you know you won't have enough for another row as you have gone past the halfway marker. Simply undo the slip knot, continue and then join in the new ball before starting the next row.

JOINING IN A NEW BALL

Whether you are joining in a new ball of the same color yarn to complete a project or joining in a different color to knit color work (pp. 136–151), the technique is the same.

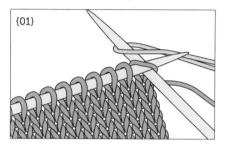

At the beginning of the row, slip the tip of the right-hand needle into the first stitch on left-hand needle in the usual way. Loop the new yarn around the tip of the right-hand needle.

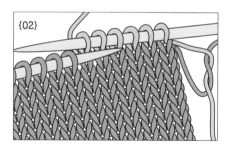

Work the next few stitches, then tie the two ends together using a single knot. When you have finished the knitting, you will weave the ends in (p. 152).

CORRECTING MISTAKES

If you are new to knitting, you are likely to make some mistakes as you learn. Don't feel despondent about this—the best knitters get it wrong from time to time. Here are some tips on correcting a few common mistakes. Remember that the sooner you spot the mistake, the easier and quicker it is to put it right.

TWISTED STITCHES

Stitches, whether they are knit or purl, should always sit on the needle with the right-hand (or front) loop coming over the front of the needle. If the left-hand (or back) loop is over the front of the needle, then the stitch is twisted. Work up to the twisted stitch, then slip it onto the right-hand needle and then back onto the left-hand needle the right way round. If you were to knit or purl a twisted stitch it would show quite clearly in the finished fabric.

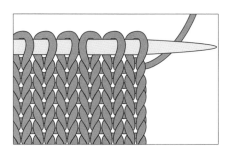

INCOMPLETE STITCHES

A common problem when learning knit and purl is working incomplete stitches. If at the end of a row you have more stitches than you started with, this is probably the cause. They usually occur when you wrap the yarn around the needle but fail to bring it through the stitch being worked into. It is easy to identify and fix an incomplete stitch.

INCOMPLETE STITCHES ON A KNIT ROW

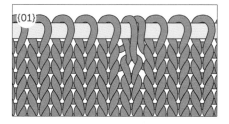

Here, the fourth stitch from the right is incomplete. The incomplete stitch was made on the previous purl row. It looks a bit like a yarnover (p. 130) followed by a slip stitch (p. 108).

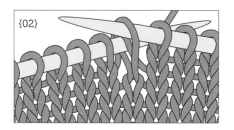

Knit to the incomplete stitch. Put the tip of the right-hand needle into the back of the "slipped" stitch on the left-hand needle. Lift this over the "yarnover" and off the needle. The stitch has been completed and is ready to be knitted in the row you are working.

INCOMPLETE STITCHES ON A PURL ROW

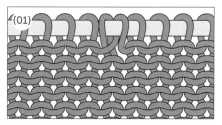

Here, the fifth stitch from the right is incomplete. The incomplete stitch was made on the previous knit row. Again, it looks a bit like a yarnover followed by a slip stitch.

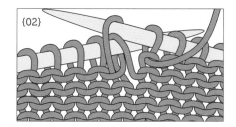

Purl to the incomplete stitch. Put the tip of the right-hand needle into the front of the "slipped" stitch on the left-hand needle. Lift this over the "yarnover" and off the needle. The stitch has been completed and is ready to be purled in the row you are working.

DROPPED STITCHES

Don't panic if you notice a dropped stitch. Keep a safety pin pinned to your knitting bag and slip it through the dropped stitch to stop it unraveling further.

ONE ROW DOWN ON A KNIT ROW

If the stitch has dropped down by one row, so there is one loose horizontal strand with it, then use this technique.

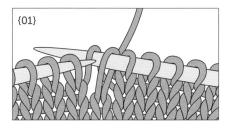

With the loose horizontal strand behind the dropped stitch, put the tip of the right-hand needle into the front of the dropped stitch and then under the horizontal strand behind it.

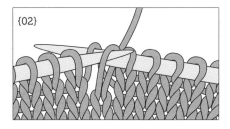

Put the tip of the left-hand needle into the back of the dropped stitch and lift it over the horizontal strand. Slip the picked-up stitch onto the left-hand needle, making sure it is not twisted.

ONE ROW DOWN ON A PURL ROW

On a purl row, the principle is the same but you are working from the other side of the knitted fabric.

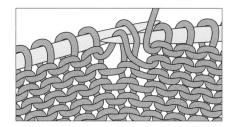

With the loose horizontal strand in front of the dropped stitch, put the tip of the right-hand needle into the back of the dropped stitch and then under the strand. Use the left-hand needle to lift the dropped stitch up and over the horizontal strand, then slip the picked-up stitch onto the left-hand needle, making sure it is not twisted.

MULTIPLE ROWS DOWN

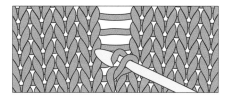

If the dropped stitch is a few rows down, you can use a crochet hook to pull the horizontal strands through the dropped stitch row by row until you reach the top.

UNRAVELING WORK

Sometimes you have to unravel the work to correct a mistake. If the mistake is just a few stitches back, unravel stitch by stitch. If it is a few rows back, then you will have to pull out the rows down to the mistake then pick up the stitches again. If you are worried about going down further than the right row, thread a tapestry needle with a contrast color yarn. Slip the needle through the right-hand (front) loop of each stitch in the row below the one that has the mistake in it. This yarn is now holding all the stitches safely while you unravel your work.

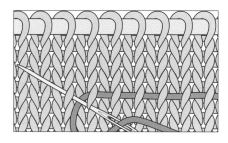

Note

If you have to turn the work to pick up a dropped stitch, when you are ready to start knitting again make sure that the working yarn is attached to the last stitch on the right-hand needle. If it is on the left-hand needle, you will be knitting in the wrong direction, a surprisingly easy thing to do.

BINDING OFF
(UK CASTING OFF)

Once you have completed your piece of work you need to finish the stitches so you can take out the needles without the knitting unraveling. This is called binding off. When binding off you use the same yarn and needles as for the work and either a knit stitch or a purl stitch, depending on whether the row would have been knitted or purled if the work were continued.

A knitwise bound off edge lies flat on the stockinette stitch side of the work.

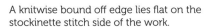

BINDING OFF KNITWISE

This is the first, and most straightforward, way of binding off that you need to learn.

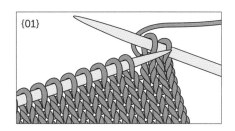

Knit the first two stitches in the usual way (p. 100).

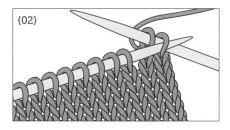

Slip the tip of the left-hand needle into the first stitch you knitted onto the right-hand needle. Lift it over the second stitch you knitted and drop it off the needle. You now have only one stitch on the right-hand needle.

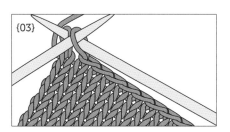

Knit another stitch from the left-hand needle and then pass the previous stitch you knitted over it. Continue in this way until you have one stitch remaining on the right-hand needle.

Cut the yarn, leaving a 6in (15cm) tail to weave in later (p. 152). Put the cut end through the remaining stitch and pull it tight.

BINDING OFF PURLWISE

This is essentially the same as binding off knitwise, but you are working with purl stitches.

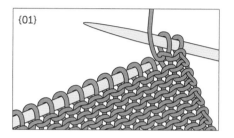

Purl the first two stitches in the usual way (p. 101).

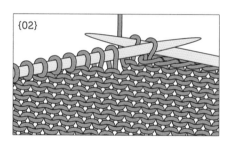

Take the yarn to the back. Slip the tip of the left-hand needle into the first stitch you purled onto the right-hand needle. Lift it over the second stitch you purled and drop it off the needle. You now have only one stitch on the right-hand needle. Continue in this way across the row. When you have only one stitch remaining, cut the yarn, leaving a 6in (15cm) tail to weave in later (p. 152). Put the cut end through the remaining stitch and pull it tight.

Note

You will often find that the last stitch on the bound off row forms an ugly, baggy point. To fix this, when binding off knitwise, work to the last stitch to be bound off: you will have one stitch on the right-hand needle and one stitch on the left-hand needle. When you come to knit the last stitch, put the tip of the needle through the same stitch on the row below. Wrap the yarn around the tip of the right-hand needle and pull the loop through the stitch, slipping the original off the needle in the usual way. Bind off the last stitch and cut the yarn and put it through the loop in the usual way. As you pull it tight, give a little wiggle and you will see that you are not left with that unsightly point. The same principle applies when binding off purlwise.

BINDING OFF IN PATTERN

Binding off in pattern creates an edge that fits in with the rest of the fabric. The technique is shown here for the working of single rib stitch, but the principles apply to all stitch patterns.

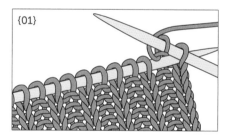

Knit one stitch, then purl one stitch. Once you have two stitches on the right-hand needle, pass the first stitch worked over the second one. After working a purl stitch, make sure the yarn is at the back before lifting the previous stitch over it.

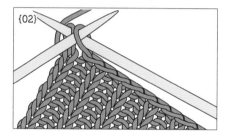

Continue across all stitches until one stitch remains, knitting the knit stitches and purling the purl ones. Cut the yarn, leaving a 6in (15cm) tail to weave in later (p. 152). Put the end through the remaining stitch and pull it tight.

Note

If you find that your bound off edge is much tighter than your knitted fabric, try binding off using a needle that is one size larger to give the edge more elasticity.

BINDING OFF TWO EDGES TOGETHER

This is a great technique for making a smooth seam, with the two knitted edges being joined together during binding off rather than having to be sewn. You need three knitting needles the same size to work this technique. It is usually worked with the right sides of both pieces together to create a subtle seam, as shown, but you can also work it wrong sides together to create a decorative feature of the seam on the right side of the fabric.

The bottom edges of the Swiss Darning Phone Covers (p. 34) are bound off together to join them.

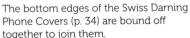

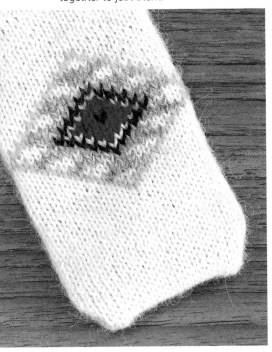

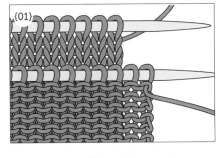

{01}

With the right sides of the work together, hold both needles, facing the same direction, in your left hand.

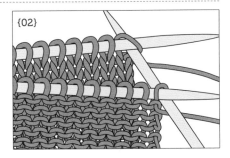

{02}

Hold a third needle in your right hand. Put the point of the right-hand needle into the back of the first stitch on the front left-hand needle and then into the front of the first stitch on the back left-hand needle.

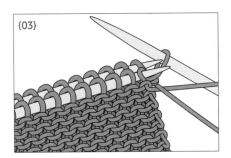

{03}

Squeezing together the two needles in the left hand, knit the two stitches together in a similar way to k2tog (p. 118). Repeat steps 2–3 again so that you have two stitches on the right-hand needle.

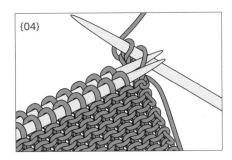

{04}

Using the tip of one of the left-hand needles, pass the first stitch on the right-hand needle over the second stitch and drop the stitch off the needle as if you were binding off in the usual way. Repeat the process until you have just one stitch on the right-hand needle. Cut the yarn, leaving a 6in (15cm) tail to weave in later (p. 152). Put the end through the remaining stitch and pull it tight.

Shaping knitted pieces

To knit a project that is more complicated than a square or rectangle, you need to learn shaping techniques. Increasing and decreasing are the main methods of shaping (although they can also be used for decorative effects such as bobbles, p. 131). Other shaping techniques include picking up stitches and short-row shaping.

INCREASING

To increase stitches is to create more of them on your needle, thus making the knitting wider. Different increases slope in different directions in the knitting, as noted for each technique as described. This is important if you want to mirror your increases at each end of a row for neatness.

Stitches made in the middle of knit rows.

MAKE ONE PATTERN ABBREVIATION: M1

Note: Slopes to the left on stockinette stitch.
When you are asked to make a stitch in this way it is usually in the middle of a row. The increase is not obvious in the finished knitting.

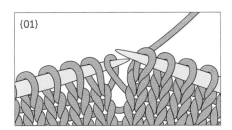

{01}

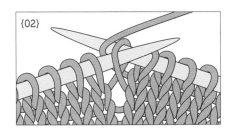

{02}

Work to the position of the increase. If you pull the tips of the needles apart slightly, you will see that there is a horizontal strand of yarn lying between the last stitch on the right-hand needle and the first on the left-hand needle. From the front, slip the tip of the right-hand needle under this strand and lift it onto the tip of the left-hand needle. Remove the right-hand needle, leaving the strand on the left-hand needle.

Knit through the back of the loop on the left-hand needle. You have made a completely new stitch and so increased by one stitch.

Note
If you want to make a stitch and have it slope to the right instead, then pick up the strand from the back and knit into the front of it. The principle is the same on a purl row.

INCREASING ONE KNITWISE   PATTERN ABBREVIATION: KFB OR INC

Note: Slopes to the left on stockinette stitch.

This is the most commonly used type of increase. It is best used on an edge as the increased stitch has a small but visible bar across it: this will disappear into the seam when the project is sewn up. Used at the beginning of a row, as shown, the increased edge slopes to the right, but the stitch itself slopes to the left.

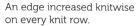
An edge increased knitwise on every knit row.

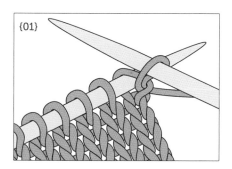

Work to the position of the increase. Knit into the front of the next stitch (p. 100), but do not slip the original stitch off the left-hand needle.

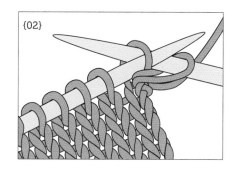

Put the tip of the right-hand needle into the back of the same stitch on the left-hand needle.

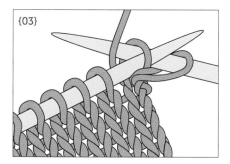

Wrap the yarn around the right-hand needle in the same way you usually would to knit a stitch.

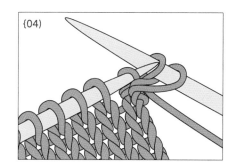

Bring the needle, and the yarn wrapped around it, through the stitch and now slip the original stitch off the left-hand needle. You have made two stitches out of one and so increased by one stitch.

Note

This style of increase is often abbreviated as inc, whether it is on a knit or a purl row. Simply use the knit technique on a knit row and the purl technique on a purl row.

INCREASING ONE PURLWISE PATTERN ABBREVIATION: PFB OR INC

Note: Slopes to the right on stockinette stitch.
The way the yarn has to twist around makes this look trickier than it actually is. Again, this is an increase usually used on an edge that will disappear into a seam. Used at the beginning of a row, as shown, the increased edge slopes to the left, but the stitch itself slopes to the right.

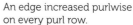
An edge increased purlwise on every purl row.

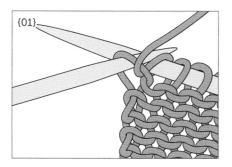

Work to the position of the increase. Purl into the front of the next stitch (p. 101), but do not slip the original stitch off the left-hand needle.

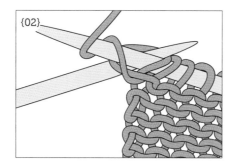

Put the tip of the right-hand needle into the back of the same stitch on the left-hand needle. Wrap the yarn around the right-hand needle as you usually would to purl a stitch.

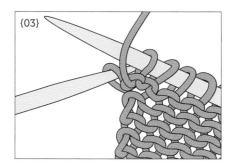

Bring the needle, and the yarn wrapped around it, through the stitch and now slip the original stitch off the left-hand needle. You have made two stitches out of one and so increased by one stitch.

You can increase multiple stitches at a time by casting on extra stitches, such as when creating the daisy petals for the Knitted Flower Bouquet (p. 24). The daisy centers and roses are shaped using the increase one knitwise technique.

DECREASING

Decreasing is the process of reducing the number of stitches on the knitting needle. Different decreases slope in different directions in the knitting, as noted for each technique as described. This is important if you want to mirror your decreases at each end of a row for neatness.

An edge decreased on every knit row.

KNIT TWO STITCHES TOGETHER PATTERN ABBREVIATION: K2TOG

Note: Slopes to the right on stockinette stitch.

This is the most basic of the decreases and the most commonly used. You would usually use it at the beginning or end of a row if the edge is to be seamed. Used at the beginning of a row, as shown, the decreased edge slopes to the left, but the stitch itself slopes to the right.

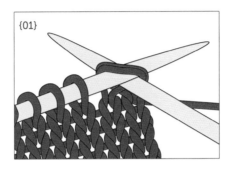

From front to back, put the tip of the right-hand needle into the next two stitches on the left-hand needle.

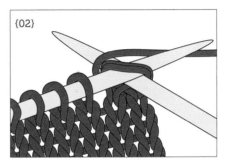

Knit the two stitches together as if they were one. You have made two stitches into one and so decreased by one stitch.

The Christmas Tree Decoration (p. 14) is shaped by knitting two stitches together at the side edges.

Note

You can knit or purl more than two stitches together at a time to decrease by more than one stitch. This applies to knitting or purling the stitches together in the standard way and also to working them together through the back loops.

PURL TWO STITCHES TOGETHER PATTERN ABBREVIATION: P2TOG

Note: Slopes to the right on stockinette stitch.

This version of the basic decrease is used when working a purl row.

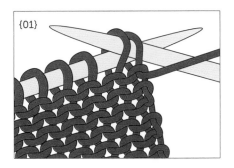

Put the tip of the right-hand needle into the next two stitches on the left-hand needle purlwise.

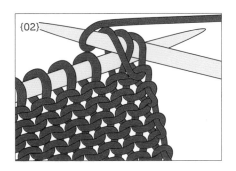

Purl the two stitches together as one. You have made two stitches into one and so decreased by one stitch.

Note

Increases and decreases are often worked several stitches in from the edges of the knitting so that they will be a visible feature when the knitting is sewn up.

An edge decreased on every purl row.

Purling two stitches together is used to make buttonholes on the Fair Isle Hot Water Bottle Cover (p. 76).

SLIP ONE, KNIT ONE, PASS THE SLIPPED STITCH OVER
PATTERN ABBREVIATION: SKPO

Note: Slopes to the left on stockinette stitch.

This technique is often used when working lace stitches (p. 129).

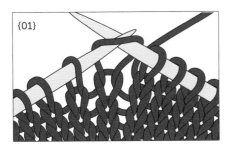

{01}

Put the tip of the right-hand needle into the next stitch and slip it knitwise (see p. 108) onto the right-hand needle.

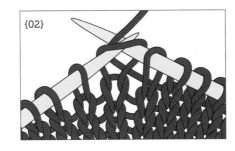

{02}

Knit the next stitch in the usual way (p. 100).

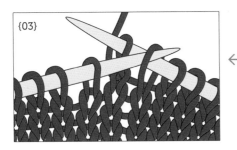

{03}

Put the tip of the left-hand needle into the front of the slipped stitch on the right-hand needle and lift it over the stitch just knitted. You have made two stitches into one and so decreased by one stitch.

Skpo used to decrease on every knit row.

The shaping of the ears on the Kawaii Kittens (p. 66) uses the skpo technique.

SLIP, SLIP, KNIT
PATTERN ABBREVIATION: SSK

Note: Slopes to the left on stockinette stitch.

This technique produces a decrease that is slightly flatter than skpo.

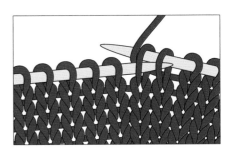

One at a time, slip the first and second stitches knitwise (see p. 108) onto your right-hand needle. From the left, put your left-hand needle into the fronts of these slipped stitches and then knit them together.

Ssk used to decrease on every knit row.

KNIT TWO STITCHES TOGETHER THROUGH THE BACKS OF THE LOOPS
PATTERN ABBREVIATION: K2TOG TBL

Note: Slopes to the left on stockinette stitch.

This is similar to k2tog (p. 118) but you are knitting through the backs of the loops (p. 107), which causes the decrease to slope in the opposite direction.

K2tog (p. 118) and k2tog tbl are combined to create the symmetrical sloping lines of shaping on Rudolph the Reindeer's head (p. 54).

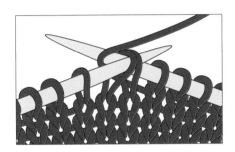

Put the tip of your right-hand needle into the backs of the first two stitches on your left-hand needle and knit these two stitches together as one. You will have made two stitches into one and so decreased by one stitch.

An edge decreased on every knit row.

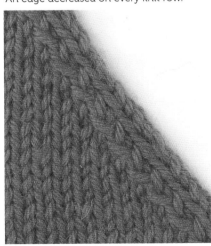

PURL TWO STITCHES TOGETHER THROUGH THE BACKS OF THE LOOPS
PATTERN ABBREVIATION: P2TOG TBL

Note: Slopes to the left on stockinette stitch.

When purling two stitches together you need to go through the backs of the loops to make the decrease slant to the left. Note that when it is used at the beginning of a row, as shown below, the decreased edge slopes to the right, but the stitch itself slopes to the left.

An edge decreased on every purl row.

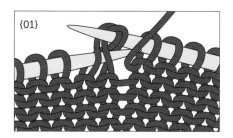

From the back to the front, put the tip of the right-hand needle into the next two stitches on the left-hand needle.

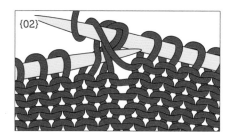

Purl the two stitches together as one. You have made two stitches into one and so decreased by one stitch.

Note

If you find it difficult to put the needle through the backs of the stitches, then put the needle into the front of the stitches first and stretch them slightly.

SLIP ONE, KNIT TWO TOGETHER, PASS THE SLIPPED STITCH OVER   PATTERN ABBREVIATION: SL1, K2TOG, PSSO

Note: Slopes to the left on stockinette stitch.

This technique enables you to decrease by two stitches at the same time and would usually be used in the middle of a row.

There are two stitches between each decrease across the row.

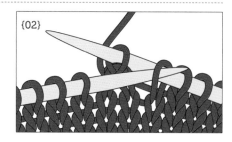

Slip the next stitch knitwise onto the right-hand needle, then knit the following two stitches together (p. 118).

Pass the slipped stitch over the two stitches knitted together. You have made three stitches into one and so decreased by two stitches.

PICK UP AND KNIT

There will be times when you have to pick up a number of stitches from a finished piece of knitting in order to knit another part of the project. For example, you can use this method when making socks to pick up stitches along the sides of the heel flap, ready to work the gusset.

On the Lacy Top Socks (p. 72), stitches are picked up and knitted along each side of the heel flap to work the triangular gusset.

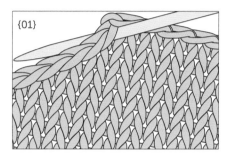

{01}

From the right side, put the tip of a needle into the space between the edge stitch and the next stitch.

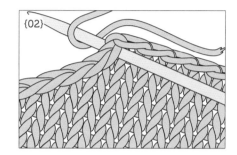

{02}

Loop the yarn around the needle. Make sure that the loop is at least 6in (15cm) from the cut end, so leaving a tail to be woven in later (p. 152).

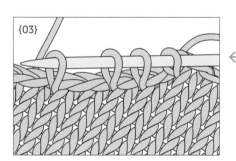

{03}

← Bring the needle, and the yarn looped around it, through the space to the front of the work. Continue in this way, picking up stitches from the finished edge as required.

SHORT-ROW SHAPING

Short-row shaping involves turning the knitting partway through a row so that you can work extra rows in a certain area of a project without binding off stitches. In some patterns this creates holes where rows are turned. To avoid this, you can use a wrap stitch technique such as the following.

WRAPPING A STITCH ON A KNIT ROW

Wrapping the stitch before you turn the work will prevent a hole forming in the fabric. This is how you do it on a knit row.

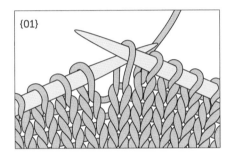

Work to the position of the turn. Slip the next stitch purlwise (p. 108) off the left-hand needle and onto the right-hand needle.

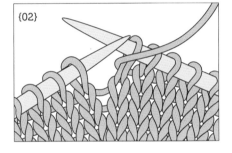

Bring the yarn forward between the two needles.

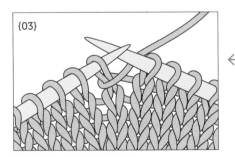

Slip the stitch back onto the left-hand needle and take the yarn to the back. The wrap lies around the base of the slipped stitch. Turn the work and work the next row as instructed in the pattern.

PICKING UP WRAPS ON A KNIT ROW

At a given point in a pattern you need to work across the row of wrapped stitches and pick up all the wraps so that they don't show on the finished project. This is how you do it on a knit row.

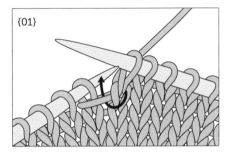

Knit to the first wrapped stitch. Put the tip of the right-hand needle up through the front of the wrap.

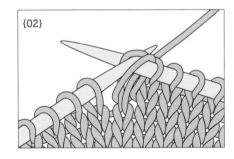

With the wrap on the needle, put the tip of this needle into the stitch it is wrapped around and knit the loop and stitch together. Continue across the row, picking up wrapped stitches as you go.

WRAPPING A STITCH ON A PURL ROW

This is how you wrap a stitch on a purl row.

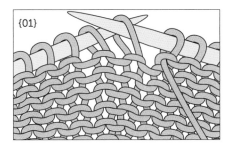

Work to the position of the turn. Slip the next stitch purlwise off the left-hand needle and onto the right-hand needle, keeping the yarn at the front of the work.

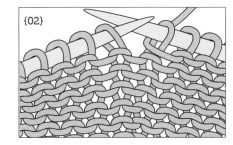

Take the yarn between the two needles to the back of the work.

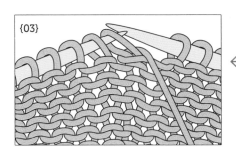

Slip the stitch back onto the left-hand needle and bring the yarn between the two needles to the front of the work. Turn the work and work the next row as instructed in the pattern.

PICKING UP WRAPS ON A PURL ROW

This is how to pick up wraps on a purl row.

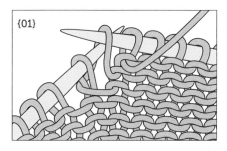

Purl to the first wrapped stitch. Using the tip of the right-hand needle, pick up the wrap from the back to the front.

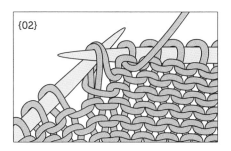

Slip the loop onto the left-hand needle and purl it together with the stitch it was wrapped around. Continue in this way across the row, picking up all the wrapped stitches as you come to them.

Note

If you pick up all of the wrapped stitches using these techniques, the wraps will almost completely disappear on the right side of the finished knitting.

The bottom point of the Zigzag Neckwarmer (p. 45) is created using short-row shaping and wrapped stitches. Always follow the wrapping method specified in the pattern as the methods can vary, although the principle remains the same.

WELTS

Welts can be used to form a three-dimensional ridge in the knitted fabric. They are usually worked in stockinette stitch, and are created by picking up stitches from a previous row and working them together with the corresponding stitches on the current row. Welts vary in depth depending on how many rows down you pick up the stitches. The tuck shown here is being worked on a knit row, but you can use the same basic technique on a purl row.

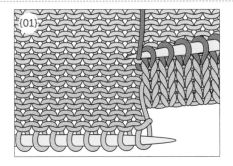

Fold the tuck fabric in half so that the wrong sides are together. Put the tip of the left-hand needle into the lower loop of the corresponding stitch on the previous row specified in the pattern. Knit (or purl) the loop together with the corresponding stitch on the current row.

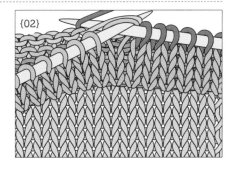

Continue in this way across the row, working corresponding stitches and loops together.

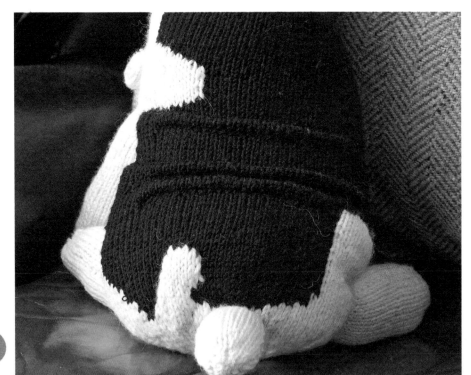

Welts are worked above the eyes and nose and on the back of the Bulldog Puppy (p. 80) to simulate folds of skin. The puppy's welts are worked on wrong-side rows and the three back welts can be seen here.

Decorative techniques

There are many ways of combining knit and purl stitches for decorative effects. Swapping groups of stitches on the needle creates cables. Increasing and decreasing can create both bobbles and deceptively complex-looking lace patterns. Loop knitting involves wrapping the yarn around your thumb—what could be simpler.

CABLES

Cables are stitches that have been lifted with a third (cable) needle and crossed to another place in the work. The results look complex but this is really quite simple to master. The cables are usually worked in stockinette stitch on a background of reverse stockinette stitch.

This cable twist is worked on every sixth row.

CABLE 4 BACK PATTERN ABBREVIATION: C4B

Holding the cable needle at the back of the work makes the cable twist across to the right.

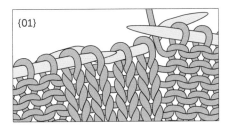

{01}

Work to the position of the cable. Slip the first two stitches from the left-hand needle onto the cable needle and leave it at the back of the work.

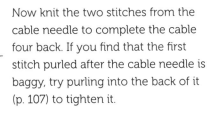

{02}

Coming in front of the cable needle that is holding the two stitches, knit the next two stitches from the left-hand needle.

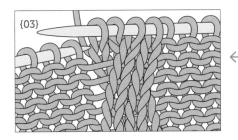

{03}

Now knit the two stitches from the cable needle to complete the cable four back. If you find that the first stitch purled after the cable needle is baggy, try purling into the back of it (p. 107) to tighten it.

CABLE 4 FRONT PATTERN ABBREVIATION: C4F

Holding the cable needle at the front of the work makes the cable twist across to the left.

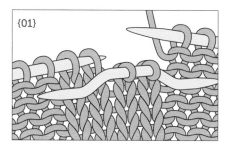

Work to the position of the cable. Slip the first two stitches from the left-hand needle onto the cable needle and leave it at the front of the work.

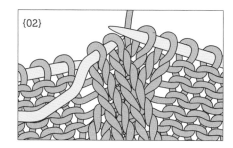

Going behind the cable needle that is holding the stitches, knit the next two stitches from the left-hand needle.

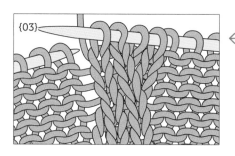

Then knit the two stitches that are on the cable needle to complete the cable.

A band of cable four front.

Note

Using a cranked cable needle like the one shown in the diagrams makes it almost impossible for the stitches to slip off while you are working the next stitches on the left-hand needle. Once you are confident with cabling, try using a straight cable needle, which makes the process a bit quicker.

Note

All cables use the techniques shown here, but they can involve different numbers of stitches. For example, "C6B" means "cable six back." You would slip three stitches onto the cable needle and hold it at the back, then knit three from the left-hand needle and finally the three from the cable needle. The pattern you are working from will tell you how many stitches to put on the cable needle and how many to knit.

The twisted pattern of the Tweed Stitch Rug (p. 28) involves working stitches out of sequence.

CROSSED AND TWISTED STITCHES

Using the same principle as cables, many other textured stitch patterns can be created by working stitches out of sequence, such as working the second stitch on the left-hand needle before working the first stitch. If it involves only one or two stitches, then a cable needle is not required.

LACE KNITTING

Lace knitting is a series of loops (demonstrated here) and decreases (p. 118) that combine to make open-work patterns. If you are tackling lace knitting for the first time it is advisable to find a pattern where every alternate row is plain knit or purl. This will make it easier if you need to unravel (p. 111) to fix a mistake.

Bringing the yarn over the needle to make a loop and a hole is known as a yarnover and it can be described in several ways. Some designers use the term "yo" for all types of yarnover; others will use different terms, depending on where the yarn has been left after the previous stitch has been worked. Here are all the different stitch combinations with specific instructions as to how to work yarnovers between them.

YARN FORWARD (YFWD)

This yarnover is used when you have just worked a knit stitch and need to do another knit stitch after the yarnover.

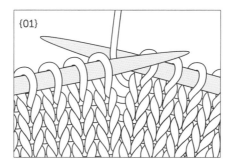

Work to the position of the yarnover. Bring the yarn forward between the tips of the needles.

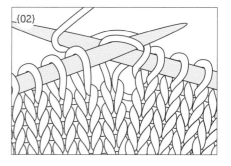

Take the yarn backward over the right-hand needle and knit the next stitch.

Yarn forward is combined with a sl1, k2tog, psso decrease (p. 122) to create the lace pattern on the Simple Lace Fingerless Mitts (p. 31).

YARN OVER NEEDLE (YON)

This yarnover is used when you have just worked a purl stitch and the following stitch will be a knit stitch.

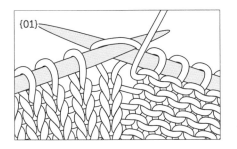

Work to the position of the yarnover. After having purled the last stitch, put the tip of the right-hand needle knitwise into the next stitch.

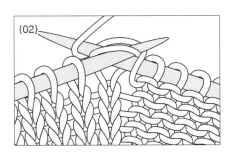

As the yarn is already at the front it will automatically go over the needle as you knit the next stitch.

YARN FORWARD ROUND NEEDLE (YFRN)

This yarnover is used when you have just worked a knit stitch and the following stitch will be a purl stitch.

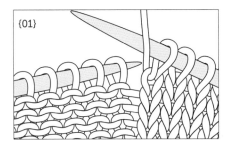

Work to the position of the yarnover. After having knitted the last stitch, bring the yarn forward between the two needles as if to purl.

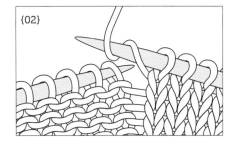

Wrap the yarn once over and around the needle until it is back in the right position to purl the next stitch.

YARN ROUND NEEDLE (YRN)

This yarnover is used when you have just worked a purl stitch and wish to do another purl stitch after the yarnover.

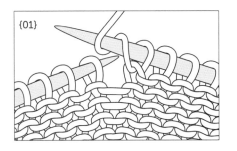

Work to the position of the yarnover. Take the yarn over the right-hand needle to the back of the work and then through between the tips of the needles and to the front of the work again.

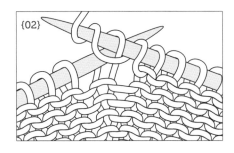

Purl the next stitch.

BOBBLES

Bobbles are a very effective textured stitch. They can differ in size and in how they are made; a pattern will give instructions for how to work the particular bobble in the project you are knitting. Bobbles are usually made in stockinette stitch. Here is a four-stitch bobble to practice your technique on.

Note

Cable and bobble stitches are sometimes referred to as Aran stitches, named for the islands off the coast of Scotland where the techniques are thought to have originated.

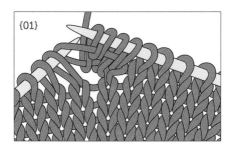

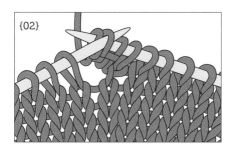

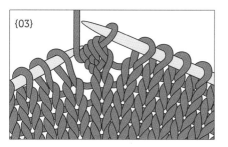

Work to the position of the bobble. In the same way as for increasing knitwise (p. 116), knit into the front, then the back, the front again, and then the back again of the next stitch, and then slip the original stitch off the left-hand needle. You have made four stitches out of one.

With the tip of the left-hand needle, lift the second stitch on the right-hand needle over the first one.

Lift the third and fourth stitches in turn over the first one. One stitch remains and the bobble is complete.

Note

If the first stitch knitted after a bobble is a little baggy, you can knit into the back of it (p. 107) to tighten it. The twisted stitch will be partly hidden by the bobble and should not show too much. Bobbles can be made with different numbers of stitches; you can also work one or more rows on the bobble stitches before working the final decrease to achieve the size of bobble you need.

A scattering of four-stitch bobbles.

LOOP KNITTING

Loop knitting can be used to lend a fur effect to knitted fabric. It can be used all over or just as an edging. Bear in mind that this technique uses a lot of yarn, approx 2in (5cm) for each loop, so if you decide to add loops to spice up a plain scarf, for example, you will need to buy more yarn than the original pattern specifies. In the diagrams the loop is shown in a different color for clarity.

Note

Loop stitch is worked on the right side of the fabric. The part of the loop where you wind the yarn around your left thumb might sound awkward, but it just takes a bit of practice. You need to hold the right-hand needle against your right palm with your second, third, and little fingers and use your right index finger and thumb to wrap the yarn around your left thumb.

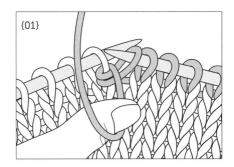

Work to the position of the loop. With the right side of the work facing you, knit the next stitch but do not allow the original stitch to drop off the left-hand needle. Bring the yarn forward between the tips of the needles to the front. Stretch out your left thumb so that it is in front of the knitting and wrap the yarn under and around it.

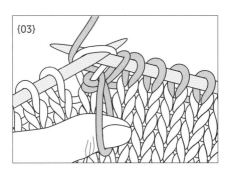

Knit into the same stitch again and then drop the original stitch off the left-hand needle. At the same time, take your left thumb out of the loop.

Loops worked on alternate stitches on knit rows.

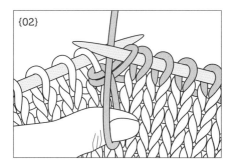

Take the yarn back between the tips of the needles to the back.

Note

If you find wrapping the yarn around your thumb a bit tricky, you can cut a strip of cardboard the desired depth of the loop and wrap the yarn around that instead.

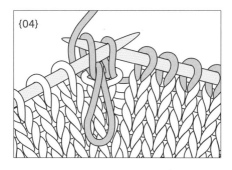

In a similar way to ssk (p. 120), put the tip of the left-hand needle through the front of the two stitches just made and knit them together. When you have finished the loop row and the next row, give all the loops a gentle tug to even them out and tighten the stitches.

Circular knitting

{ *Circular knitting, or knitting in the round, produces a seamless tube of fabric. As well as the elimination of seams, some knitters also find it an advantage that you only work on the right side of the fabric, which is always facing you. Circular knitting can be done using either a circular needle or a set of double-pointed needles.* }

CIRCULAR NEEDLE

A circular needle has two pointed ends joined with a cord, which comes in varying lengths and is usually made from plastic or nylon. A pattern should tell you which length to use.

JOINING TO WORK IN THE ROUND

When you see this phrase in a pattern, it simply means that you should start knitting the first stitch as instructed, thereby joining the first and last cast on stitches together to form a circle. There will be a small gap at the cast on edge at this joining point. There are several ways of eliminating this if you wish. A simple method is to cast on one extra stitch. Pass a stitch from the right-hand needle to the left-hand needle and then knit or purl two together (in line with the pattern being worked) to complete the circle.

WORKING IN ROUNDS

The easiest way to knit in the round is to use a circular needle. Using the two pointed tips of the needle, cast on in the usual way (pp. 95–99).

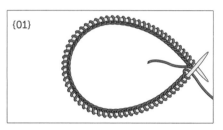

{01}

Cast on the required number of stitches and check carefully that the cast on row is not twisted around the needle. If it is, you will end up knitting a Mobius strip rather than a tube.

{02}

Place a round marker (p. 90) on the right-hand point of the needle after completing the cast on. When knitting the first stitch of the round, make sure you pull the yarn across tightly.

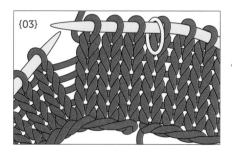

{03}

← Knit until you come to the round marker; you have completed one round. Slip the marker onto the right-hand point of the needle and start to knit the next round. Continue in this way, slipping the marker at the beginning of every round.

WORKING IN ROWS

A circular needle can also be used for knitting conventionally—back and forth in rows—by swapping the points in your hands at the end of each row. With heavy projects, such as a rug or blanket, you can cast on a lot of stitches easily and stretch them out to see how the pattern is growing. As the work progresses, you can hold the weight of the knitted fabric in your lap and not on the needles, thus sparing you aches and pains in your wrists and arms. It is very easy to travel with circular needles as they pack away neatly and if you are knitting on a train or plane (if the airline allows it), you won't nudge your traveling neighbor as you would with the ends of straight needles.

The Baby Blanket (p. 22) can be worked in rows on a circular needle.

MAGIC LOOP TECHNIQUE

The magic loop technique allows you to use a circular needle even when making small-diameter pieces such as socks, rather than having to use double-pointed needles. This technique can help to reduce the occurrence of ladders between the sets of stitches that can happen when working on double-pointed needles. You can use a round marker to mark the start of the round in the usual way.

Note

When using the magic loop technique, you will always have half the stitches on the cable of the circular needle and half being worked on the needle tips. The loop of cable between the sets of stitches lets you knit easily.

{01} Cast on the correct number of stitches according to your pattern and slide them down onto the cable of the circular needle. Find the halfway point of the stitches and pull the cable through between them so that the stitches slide up onto the two needle points. The last cast on stitch with the working yarn attached to it should be at the tip of the right-hand needle.

{02} Gently draw the needle tip and cable through the right-hand group of stitches until you have enough flexibility to knit into the first stitch on the left-hand needle. Knit (or work as instructed in your pattern) the first stitch on the left-hand needle, making sure that you pull the yarn tight from the previous stitch.

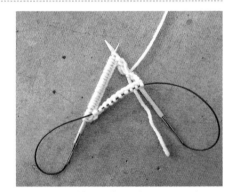

Adjust the cable until you have enough flexibility to work the stitches.

{03} Continue until all the stitches on the left-hand needle have been worked onto the right-hand needle. Then slide the second group of stitches from the cable up onto the left-hand needle, so that half of the stitches are on each needle point as before. Repeat steps 2 and 3 to continue working in rounds.

DOUBLE-POINTED NEEDLES

Double-pointed needles have a point at both ends so that you can knit from either end. They come in sets of four or five needles. Usually you would work on four needles on a small project, and for larger projects you would use five needles. The example shows four needles used.

Note

The four needles will feel awkward in your hands at first, so before you start a project, cast on some stitches using spare yarn and knit a few practice rounds. On each round, the lower tip of the left-hand needle should lie in front of the tip of the needle making up the bottom of the triangle and the lower tip of the right-hand needle should lie behind the other tip of the bottom needle.

Pull the working yarn tight when knitting (or purling) the first stitch on each double-pointed needle to help eliminate the ladders that can appear between the sets of stitches.

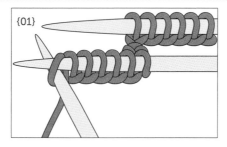

{01}

Cast on the required number of stitches onto the first needle, plus one extra stitch. Slip the extra stitch onto the second needle and then repeat the process until the required number of stitches is cast on to all three needles.

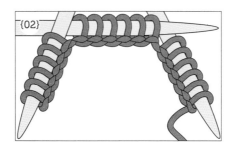

{02}

Lay out the needles with the tips overlapping as shown here. Make sure that the cast on edge faces into the middle all the way around and is not twisted at any point.

Note

Another way of getting started on double-pointed needles is to cast all of the stitches onto a single double-pointed needle, then divide them onto two other needles by slipping the first third of the stitches from the front of the first needle and the last third of the stitches from the other end of it. Some knitters prefer to cast on using standard straight needles (of the correct size), and then slip the stitches onto the three double-pointed needles.

{03}

Place a round marker (p. 90) on the needle after the last stitch has been cast on. Arrange the triangle of needles so that the first needle (the one holding the first cast on stitch) is in your left hand; the needle with the working end of the yarn will be to the right of it. Holding the free (fourth) needle in your right hand, use it to knit the stitches off the first needle. When all the stitches are knitted, the first needle becomes the free one, ready to knit the stitches off the second needle with. Continue knitting off each needle in turn until you come to the marker and then slip the marker from the left-hand needle to the right-hand needle and knit the next round.

Color work

Working with color takes your knitting to new levels. Color effects look gorgeous but it can be difficult to get the finished appearance as neat as your usual stockinette stitch. Simple color work techniques include knitting stripes and Swiss darning, while Fair Isle and intarsia allow you to create complex color designs.

KNITTING STRIPES

The easiest way to introduce color work into your knitting is by working horizontal stripes. They are simple and fun and can be added to almost any existing pattern. Vertical stripes need to be worked using the intarsia technique (p. 149).

CARRYING YARN UP THE SIDE OF THE WORK

When you are working stripes, do not join in a new color for every stripe. Instead, carry the colors not in use up the side of the work until you need them again. The colors must be caught into the knitting at the end of every alternate row to prevent big loops appearing.

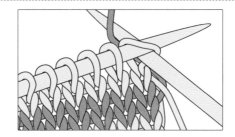

If you are working a two-row stripe, just knit the first stitch of the third row with the new color. For wider stripes, catch in any yarns being carried up the side at the start of the next row. Put the right-hand needle into the first stitch, lay the yarn to be carried over the working yarn and work the first stitch in the working yarn.

JOINING IN A NEW COLOR STRIPE

You can simply join in a new color at the side seam (p. 109), but to eliminate some of the ends at the side it is best to join in the new color before the end of the last row of the old color. This technique leaves you with fewer ends to weave in when the knitting is complete.

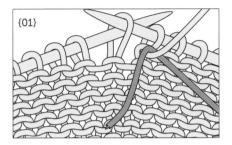

{01}

On the row before the new color is needed, stop about ten stitches before the end of the row. Lay the new color over the existing color.

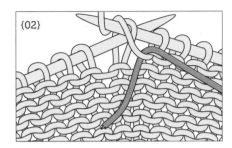

{02}

Hold the new color down with your left thumb and work the next stitch in the existing color, catching the new color into the back of the stitch.

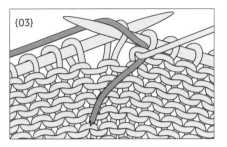

{03}

To weave the new color in as you work, lay it over the tip of the right-hand needle.

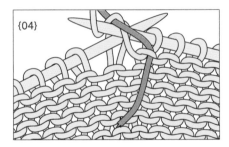

{04}

Work the next stitch using the existing color and keeping the new color held high to stop it from going through the stitch.

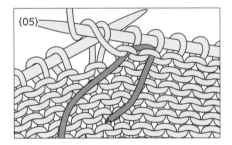

{05}

Holding the new color down, work the next stitch with the existing color. Continue in this way, weaving in the new color on every alternate stitch to the end of the row. Turn the work and the new color is safely secured and ready to do the next row. If you no longer need the old color, cut the end and weave it in on the following row on every alternate stitch.

The Elf Christmas Tree Decoration (p. 15) is a fun way to begin to practice changing colors.

DIFFERENT STRIPE EFFECTS

It's very easy to be really creative with stripes. You just need to use your imagination a little when it comes to choosing colors, stitches, and stripe widths. Here are three different stripe samplers you can try to give you some ideas.

STRIPES
Using shades A and B and working in st st throughout.
Rows 1–4: A.
Rows 5–8: B.
Rows 9–12: A.
Repeat rows 5–12.

UNEVEN STRIPES
Using shades A and B and working in st st throughout.
Rows 1–3: A.
Rows 4–5: B.
Rows 6–9: A.
Repeat rows 4–9.

TEXTURE STRIPES
Using shades A, B, C, and D and working in st st unless otherwise stated.
Rows 1–4: A.
← **Row 5**: B.
Row 6: C.
Rows 7–10: C in seed stitch.
Row 11: B.
Rows 12–15: D.
Row 16: B.
Row 17: C.
Rows 18–20: C in seed stitch.
Row 21: B.
Repeat these 21 rows.

WORKING STRIPES OVER AN ODD NUMBER OF ROWS

If the stripes are over an odd number of rows, the next time you need a specific color it will be at the wrong side of the work. Rather than joining in the new color (p. 137), work back and forth on a circular needle and when the yarn is at the wrong end, simply slide your stitches to the other end of the needle and turn the work and the right color will be there ready to knit with. If you are not working on a circular needle and the yarn you need is at the wrong end, slip the stitches back onto the left-hand needle, then start the next row. Remember to carry the yarn up both sides of the work.

On the Seed Stitch Stripy Cushion (p. 51), a single row of seed stitch at the beginning of each stripe adds textural interest.

SWISS DARNING

Also known as duplicate stitch, Swiss darning resembles knit stitches and can be used to embroider small areas of color detail without all the fuss of knitting with several colors. It may also be used to hide a mistake in your color knitting. For the best results, work Swiss darning in a yarn that is the same weight and texture as that used to knit the project.

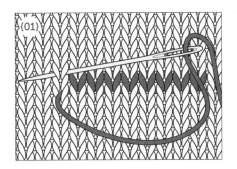

To work a horizontal row of Swiss darning, work from right to left across the knitted fabric. Bring the needle through from the back of the knitted fabric at the base of a stitch, then take it under the two loops at the base of the stitch above.

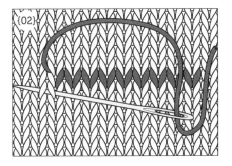

Put the needle back through to the back of the fabric where it first came out at the base of the lower stitch and take it across to come out at the base of the next stitch to the left. One Swiss-darned stitch is complete.

Note

To start embroidery, do not knot the end of the yarn as it will probably just pull through the fabric. Instead, weave the needle and yarn back and forth through a few knitted stitches on the back of the fabric, underneath the area that will be covered by the embroidery stitches. To fasten off after finishing the stitching, either weave in as before or, if the stitch permits, weave the end into the back of the embroidery, being careful not to pull it too tight and so distort the stitching on the right side of the work.

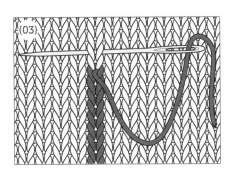

To work a vertical row, work from bottom to top of the knitted fabric. Bring the needle through the base of a stitch and take it under the loops of the stitch above, as before. Take it back through the base of the stitch and then bring it to the front through the base of the stitch above.

The color work on this phone cover is applied using Swiss darning (see Swiss Darning Phone Covers, p. 34).

FAIR ISLE

Fair Isle is a type of color knitting where you are working with two or more colors in stockinette stitch and the pattern is a repetitive design. Yarns that are not being used have to be carried (or stranded, as it is known) across the back of the work, thus making the fabric double thickness. The art of good Fair Isle is to keep the fabric elastic and supple; to achieve this you must be very careful not to pull the yarns too tightly. When worked properly the yarns should not tangle.

The front of a piece of Fair Isle knitting.

JOINING IN A NEW COLOR

When working Fair Isle, it is better to join in a new color at the beginning of a row, but if you have to join it in mid row, this is how to do it, first on a knit row (steps 1 and 2) and then on a purl row (step 3).

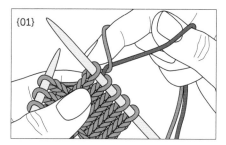

{01}

On a knit row, lay the new color (B, purple) over the original color (A, green). Twist the yarns over themselves and hold them in place.

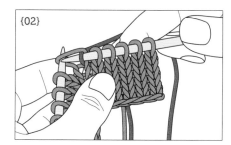

{02}

Knit with the new color (B). You can always go back and tighten the join after a couple of stitches.

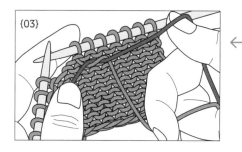

{03}

On a purl row, lay the new color (B, purple) over the original color (A, green). Twist the yarns over themselves and hold them in place. Purl with the new color (B).

Note

Once you have joined in the yarns, there are three possible techniques to use when knitting in Fair Isle and they all take practice to master. The techniques differ in whether you hold the yarns only in your right hand or in both hands; you should choose the method you find most comfortable. Whichever technique you use, it is advisable to only strand the yarn across the back for a maximum of three stitches. If the design requires you to carry the yarn for more than three stitches then you need to catch (or weave) the yarn into the back of the work. If you do not do this you will end up with large loops that may snag. You will also tend to pull the strands too tight and this will cause the work to pucker on the front.

HOLDING YARNS ONE AT A TIME

With this technique you are holding just one of the different colored yarns in your right hand at any one time. This is the simplest yet slowest of the Fair Isle techniques.

ON A KNIT ROW

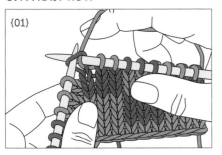

Knit the stitches as usual in yarn A (green).

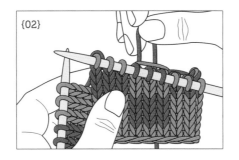

Drop yarn A and pick up yarn B (purple), making sure yarn B comes under yarn A.

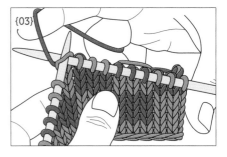

Knit with yarn B in the usual way, but be sure not to pull the yarn too tight.

ON A PURL ROW

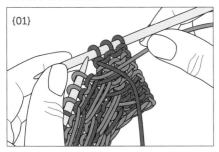

Purl the stitches as usual in yarn B (purple). Drop B and pick up yarn A (green), making sure A comes under B.

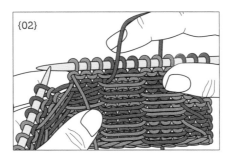

To change colors back to yarn B (purple), drop A and bring B across over yarn A.

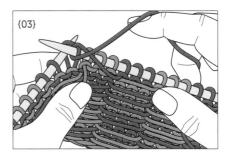

Purl with yarn B in the usual way.

Note
Keep the stitches on the right-hand needle spread out; this will help stop you pulling the yarns too tightly as you carry them across the back.

HOLDING BOTH YARNS IN YOUR RIGHT HAND

Once mastered, this is a speedier technique than holding one yarn at a time (see p. 141).

ON A KNIT ROW

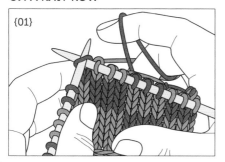

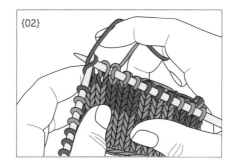

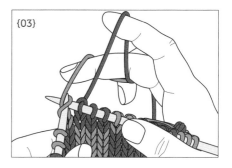

Put the tip of the right-hand needle into the stitch and place both yarns in your right hand. Place the yarn to be used first over your index finger and the other over your second finger.

Using your index finger, knit the number of stitches required in that color yarn.

Using your second finger, knit the stitches in the other color, making sure that the yarn comes up from under the first yarn knitted with.

ON A PURL ROW

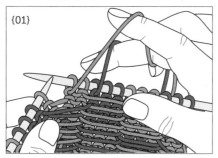

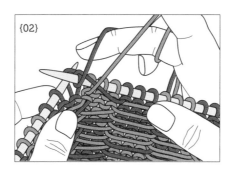

Note
If your Fair Isle knitting is very tight, go up a needle size in order to obtain the correct gauge.

Place the yarns in your right hand as you would for working a knit row. Purl the required number of stitches using the yarn that is held over your index finger.

Alternate fingers as the different-colored yarns are needed.

HOLDING YARNS IN BOTH HANDS

This technique is usually the hardest to master, but once you can work it you can knit Fair Isle very quickly and evenly.

ON A KNIT ROW

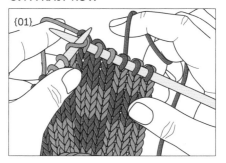

Place the yarn to be used first (A, purple) in your right hand and the other (B, green) over the index finger of your left hand. Turn to Continental Method (pp. 102–103) to see how best to hold the yarn and knit the stitches with your left hand.

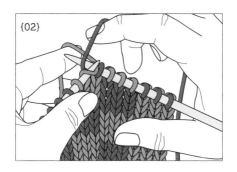

Knit the required number of stitches with your right hand and yarn A.

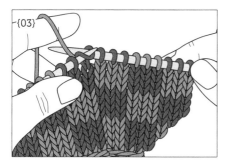

When yarn B is needed, simply place the right-hand needle over yarn B.

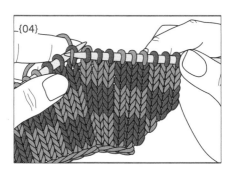

Bring the stitch through.

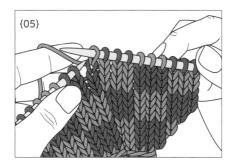

Complete the stitch, keeping yarn B on your left hand.

ON A PURL ROW

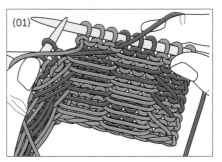

Hold yarn B (green) in your left hand and yarn A (purple) in your right hand.

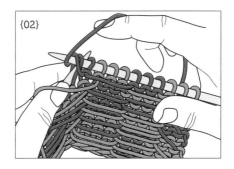

Purl in yarn A, keeping yarn B over your left thumb.

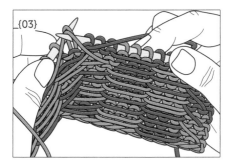

When yarn B is needed, place the right-hand needle under yarn B.

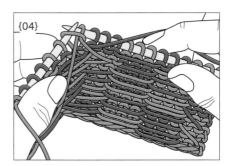

Push the stitch through. Complete the stitch, keeping yarn B on your left hand.

The design around the top of the Zigzag Neckwarmer (p. 45) is a simple introduction to the Fair Isle technique.

STRANDING YARNS USING THE RIGHT-HAND TECHNIQUE

If you work Fair Isle with your right hand (pp. 141–142), use the right-hand technique for stranding. On the examples shown in the diagrams there are five stitches between the colors, so you would need to catch in the yarn on the third stitch of the five.

ON A KNIT ROW

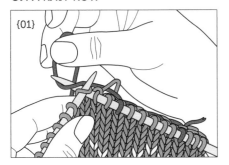

Knit to the right stitch. Drop yarn A (green) and pick up B (purple), making sure you pass it under A, and place B over the tip of the right-hand needle.

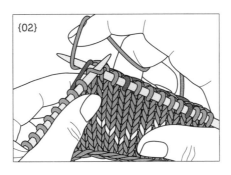

Lay yarn B across the left-hand needle and knit using yarn A.

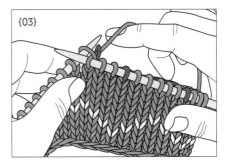

Make sure that you do not bring yarn B through the stitch as well as yarn A.

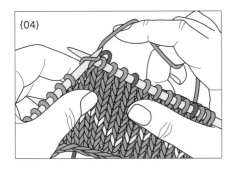

Knit the next stitch to lock the strand into place.

Note

When you have to strand the yarn across more than three stitches before being used again, you have to catch (or weave) the yarn into the back of the work to avoid long loops of yarn that can get snagged. There are two ways of doing this; the technique you choose will depend on how you hold the yarns when working Fair Isle, using the right-hand only (pp. 141–142) or using both hands (pp. 143–144).

ON A PURL ROW

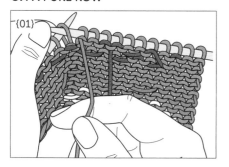

Purl to the right stitch. Hold yarn A (green) down at the back of the fabric.

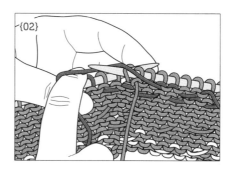

Bring yarn B across, over the right-hand needle, and lay it across the left-hand needle.

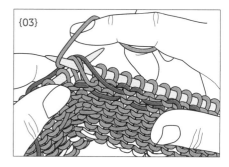

Purl using yarn A.

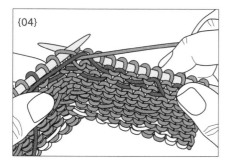

Make sure yarn B doesn't come through the stitch as well. Purl the next stitch to lock the strand into place.

Note

You can't catch in the yarn on the last stitch of a row or the stitch before you need the color. Stranded yarns need a following stitch to lock them in place.

The back of a piece of Fair Isle knitting showing the stranded yarns.

STRANDING YARNS HOLDING YARNS IN BOTH HANDS

Use this method if you use both hands to knit Fair Isle (pp. 143–144). In the diagrams, the yarn is being caught into the third stitch of a group of five that it has to go across.

ON A KNIT ROW

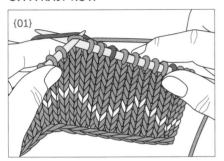

{01}

Hold the yarns in both hands as for two-handed Fair Isle, making sure the yarn being stranded is in your left hand. Knit to the right stitch then place the right-hand needle under yarn B (purple) on your left hand.

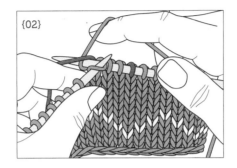

{02}

Knit the stitch with yarn A (green) in your right hand.

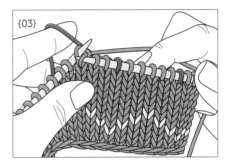

{03}

Make sure yarn B doesn't come through the stitch as well.

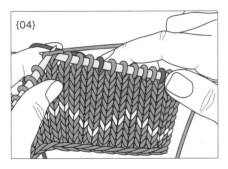

{04}

Knit the next stitch to lock the strand into place.

The @ symbol on the Intarsia iPad Case (p. 58) is worked using the Fair Isle technique, and you can see the yarns stranded across the reverse of the fabric. By contrast, the remainder of the design is worked using the intarsia technique (p. 149).

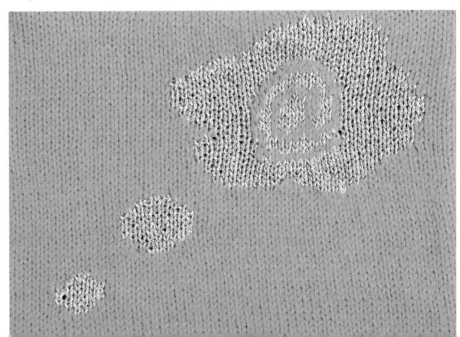

ON A PURL ROW

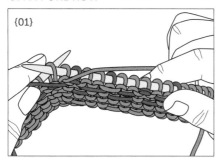

{01}

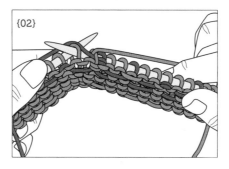

{02}

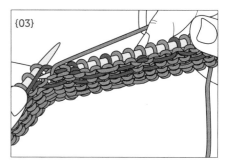

{03}

Hold the yarns as for stranding with both hands on a knit row (see p. 147) and purl to where you need to catch in the yarn.

Place the right-hand needle under yarn B (purple) held in your left hand.

Purl with yarn A (green), making sure yarn B stays in front and doesn't go through the stitch. Purl the next stitch to lock the strand into place.

Note

When stranding yarn on a repetitive design it is easy to catch it in to the back of the same stitch on each row, but try not to do this as it will cause ridges on the front of the work. If you caught the yarn into the third stitch of a group of five on one row, catch it into the second stitch of the group on the next row.

The Fair Isle Hot Water Bottle Cover (p. 76) looks complex, but you will only need to catch in the stranded yarns on the central band of the design.

INTARSIA

Intarsia is the term used for knitting blocks of pattern that require separate balls of yarn for each area of the color, and the fabric remains single thickness throughout. You have to join the areas of color that are next to each other as you work.

Purchased bobbins are usually made of plastic and you wind the amount of yarn required around them. Take care that they do not catch on each other. If you are using quite a bulky yarn you won't be able to get very much on them, so hand-made bobbins may be a better option.

BOBBINS

Bobbins keep the yarns organized when working with several colors. If you work with whole balls, the yarns will twist and tangle. There are two types of bobbin: purchased (usually made of plastic) and handmade. Instructions are given here for making a handmade bobbin.

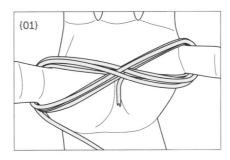

{01}

With the tail of the yarn in your palm, wrap the working end in a figure-of-eight pattern around your thumb and little finger.

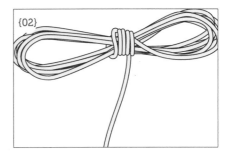

{02}

When you have enough yarn wrapped (see How Much Yarn), slip the bundle off your hand and wrap the tail end tightly around the center to tie the bundle together. Make sure that the free end sticks out of the bundle.

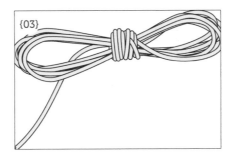

{03}

When you use the bobbin, pull the free end gently to pull the yarn from the center, making sure not to pull out too much at a time. The key to intarsia work is to keep the bobbins short at the back of the work to prevent them from tangling.

HOW MUCH YARN

To determine how much yarn to make into a bobbin for a specific area of color, work out how many stitches the area occupies; twist the yarn around your knitting needle that number of times, and add a little extra for weaving in the ends.

Note

When working a very small area of color in intarsia it is better to work with a strand of the yarn rather than a bobbin to help prevent tangling.

JOINING IN A NEW COLOR

When working in intarsia you will find yourself needing to join in a new color in the middle of a row.

The vertical stripes of the Popcorn Kitten (p. 68) can be worked using either intarsia techniques or Fair Isle (p. 140).

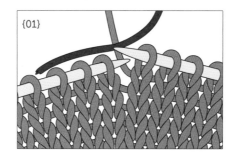

On a knit row, knit to the change in color. Lay the new color over the existing color and between the two needles, with the tail to the left.

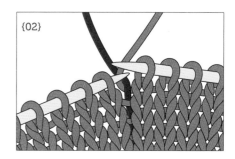

Bring the new color under and then over the existing color.

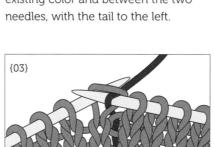

Knit the stitch with the new color. Go back and pull gently on the tail to tighten up the first stitch in the new color after you have knitted a couple more stitches.

CHANGING COLORS IN A STRAIGHT VERTICAL LINE

Once you have joined in a new color you may need to work for a number of rows changing these colors on both the knit rows and purl rows. This is often confusingly referred to as "twisting" the yarns, but it is a link rather than a twist. It is a common mistake to over-twist the yarns at this point; if you do so the fabric will not lie flat.

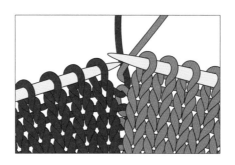

On a knit row, knit to the change in color. Bring the new color up from under the old color and drop the old color so that the new color is ready to work with.

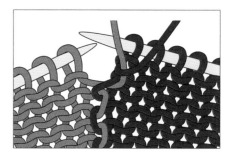

On a purl row, knit to the change in color. Bring the new color from the left under the old color and up to the top. Drop the old color and continue with the new color.

CHANGING COLORS ON THE DIAGONAL

The technique is the same as for changing colors in a straight vertical line (p. 150), but you will find that sometimes the yarn you want is in a different place; if you get the technique wrong you may end up over-twisting the yarns.

Note

When working in intarsia you will sometimes need to carry a contrast yarn across the back for a few stitches, ready for the next row where it will be needed earlier than where it was left on the previous row. You can do this by weaving in the contrast yarn along the row, using the same technique as for joining in a new color stripe (see p. 137).

Diagonal color changes are used on the Intarsia Diamonds Cushion (p. 52).

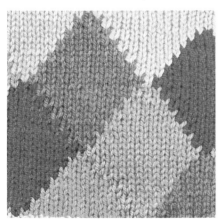

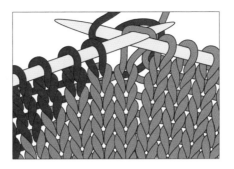

On a knit row with the diagonal going to the right, bring the new color from underneath the old color and knit with it.

On a purl row with the diagonal going to the left, bring the new color from underneath the old color and purl with it.

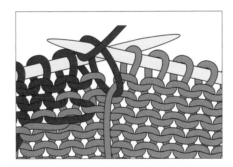

On a purl row with the diagonal going to the right, bring the new color under the old color and purl with it.

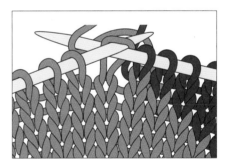

On a knit row with the diagonal going to the left, bring the new color from underneath the old color and knit with it.

Note

Some intarsia designs contain more complex sections that might be better worked using Fair Isle techniques (p. 140). This will save you having to keep swapping bobbins around and produce a neater result. Before you start such a project, spend time working out which techniques you are going to use to knit which parts of the design.

Finishing techniques

When you have put time and effort into knitting a project, it is well worth finishing it properly. Some people rush this part of a project and that is always a mistake, as careful finishing will produce a professional look. Read this section for advice on assembling your project, as well as for guidance on felting and making pom-poms.

WEAVING IN ENDS

The first step in finishing a project is to weave in (or sew in or darn in as it is sometimes known) all the ends of yarn left from casting on, binding off, and joining in new balls.

CAST ON AND BOUND-OFF ENDS

Thread a tapestry needle with the tail of yarn left over from casting on or binding off.

Note

Once you have sewn up the seams of a project, use the same techniques to weave the tails of yarn left from joining in new balls into the seams or into the edge of the knitting.

If the edge is not going to be sewn into a seam, then weave the end in and out of a few stitches along the edge of the knitting. Skipping the last stitch, weave it back through the stitches, then trim the end of the yarn tail close to the knitting.

If the edge is going to be seamed, then it is neater to weave the end into the seam allowance. To do this, first sew up the seam using the appropriate technique (pp. 154–156). Thread a tapestry needle with the tail of yarn and weave it through a few stitches in the seam allowance. Skipping the last stitch, weave it back through the stitches, then trim the end of the yarn tail close to the knitting.

INTARSIA ENDS

When you have knitted an intarsia project, you may have a lot of ends to weave in. This can be time-consuming, but you need to do it properly or the knitting will unravel. Weaving in the ends also gives you the opportunity to ease or tighten any irregular stitches at the beginning and end of a motif. Always weave ends into the backs of stitches that are the same color or you risk the wrong color showing on the front of the work.

Note

If you weave in the ends as you finish each piece of a project then it won't seem like such a huge task when all the knitting is completed.

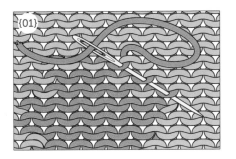

Thread a tapestry needle with one end of yarn at a time. Weave the needle into the backs of four to five stitches that are the same color as the end, making sure that you go through the yarn, splitting it, not under the stitches. This will provide extra friction and help stop the ends working free.

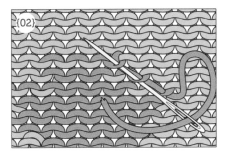

Take the needle back through two or three of the same stitches. Pull the fabric slightly to secure the end and trim it close to the knitting.

PRESSING AND BLOCKING

Pressing or blocking will improve the look of the knitted fabric and aid the sewing-up process. Do this after weaving in ends but before sewing seams. Lay the fabric right side down on a flat padded surface such as an ironing board and pin out to the correct size.

Referring to the ball band of the yarn for guidance, use an iron over a dry or damp cloth to press or steam the knitting. For delicate yarns or textured stitch patterns, block the knitting instead of using an iron. To do this, either pin out the item, spray lightly with water and allow to dry; or carefully wash the item, gently squeeze out excess water, pin out to shape and allow to dry. Whichever method you use, never unpin the knitting until completely dry.

The Simple Lace Fingerless Mitts (p. 31) should be blocked to size before making up.

SEWING SEAMS

Three methods of sewing seams are explained here to give you a variety of options for making up the projects in this book. Use safety pins to loosely pin the pieces together before you start sewing. Leave tails of yarn at the beginning and end of seams rather than use knots, then weave them in when you have finished (p. 152). Use matching color yarn; a contrasting color is used in the illustrations for clarity.

MATTRESS STITCH

Also known as ladder stitch, this technique produces an almost invisible seam. As mattress stitch is worked row by row on the right side, it is perfect for joining color work: a touch of magic when piecing stripes together. The other advantage is that if the yarn you have knitted with has too loose a twist or is too frail to sew up with, you can use another yarn of a similar color and it won't show.

SEWING STOCKINETTE STITCHES TO STITCHES

With right sides facing you, place the two pieces to be joined side by side. Thread a tapestry needle with a long length of yarn.

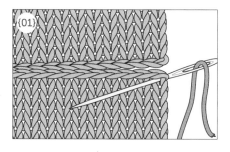

From the back, bring the tapestry needle up through the first stitch in the lower piece of knitted fabric.

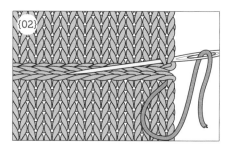

Take the needle under both loops of the same stitch on the other piece, so that it emerges between the first and second stitches.

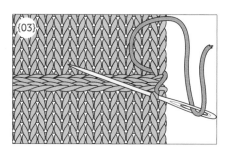

Go back into the lower piece where the needle first came out and take it under one loop, so that it emerges between the first and second stitches.

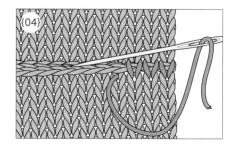

Take the needle under both loops of the second stitch on the upper piece, then under both loops of the second stitch on the lower piece. Continue in this way. When you have sewn about 2in (5cm) of the seam, gently pull the stitches up to close the seam.

SEWING STOCKINETTE STITCH ROW ENDS TO ROW ENDS

This technique will usually be used when sewing up side seams. Here it is shown worked half a stitch in from the edges, but you can work a whole stitch in if you prefer (or if your edge stitches tend to be baggy). With right sides facing you, place the two pieces of knitting to be joined side by side. Thread a tapestry needle with a long length of yarn.

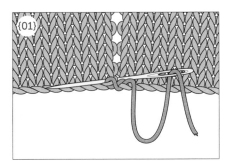

To start the seam, bring the needle from the back of the right-hand piece through the center of the first stitch of the first row. Take it across to the other piece and, from the back, bring it through the first stitch. Take it back to the first piece and, again from the back, bring it through where it first came through. Finally, take the needle through the back of the first stitch on the left-hand piece and pull tight the figure-of-eight you have made.

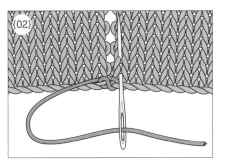

Take the needle across to the right-hand piece and, from the front, take it through the middle of the first stitch and under the bar of yarn that divides that stitch from the one above. (If the knitted fabrics are both all one color, and precise matching is not important, you can take the needle under two stitch bars at a time.)

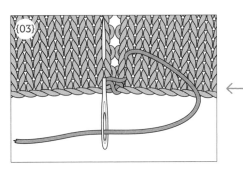

Take the needle across to the left-hand piece and, from the front, take it through the middle of the first stitch and under one (or two) bars. Continue up the seam in this way, zigzagging between the two pieces and picking up the same number of stitch bars on either side. When you have sewn about 2in (5cm) of the seam, gently pull the stitches up to close the seam and then continue.

Note

When you are working mattress stitch, on either stitches or row ends, do not pull the yarn too tightly or the seam will be very stiff. You also risk breaking the yarn and having to unpick the seam and start again.

SEWING STOCKINETTE STITCH ROW ENDS TO STITCHES

This is a combination of the techniques for sewing stitches to stitches (p. 154) and row ends to row ends (p. 155).

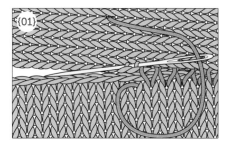

On the row end edge (top), take the needle under two bars of yarn. On the stitch edge (bottom), take the needle under both loops of each stitch.

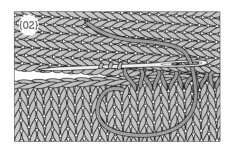

However, as a stitch is wider than it is long, on every third stitch through the row end edge, take the needle under three bars instead of two.

BACKSTITCH SEAM

This is the stitch most commonly used for joining knitting. It can sometimes make a bulky seam and it can be difficult to match patterns as backstitch is worked on the wrong side of the fabric. However, for plain stockinette stitch it is a strong, fairly quick stitch to work. Always pin the pieces together before you start to sew.

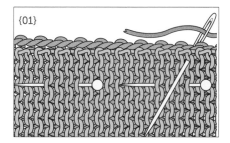

Work the backstitch one knitted stitch in from the edge. Starting on the right, bring the needle through both layers of fabric from the back to the front.

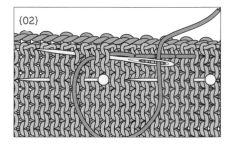

Take the needle back through the fabrics about one knitted stitch back from where it last came out and bring it back through to the front about one knitted stitch in front of where you started. Continue along the seam in this way to the end.

FLAT SEAM

A flat seam is achieved by using overstitch (also known as oversewing or overcasting). This seam is especially good for joining seed or garter stitch edges. Look carefully at the edge of seed and garter stitch and you will see a series of regularly spaced bobbles: it is these that will be stitched together.

Starting at the back of the work on the right, bring the needle through the same bobble on the edge of both pieces of fabric and pull tight. Take the needle over the top of the edges of the fabric and, from the back, go through the next bobbles on the edges. Continue along the seam, going through each pair of bobbles in turn.

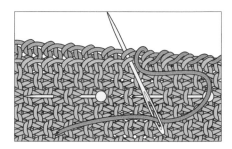

FELTING

Agitating wool yarn in hot soapy water will felt it, as anyone who has accidentally put a cashmere sweater in the hot wash will know. The hot water and soap cause the wool fibers to cling to one another and the more the item is kneaded or rubbed, the more tightly the fibers cling and the more the knitting will felt. Different effects can be achieved by mixing wool yarns, which do felt, and cotton or manmade fiber ones, which don't.

Note

Felting shrinks and thickens knitting, so pieces must be knitted larger and more loosely than usual. Even in experienced hands felting can be a trial and error process, so approach it with caution.

FELTING IN THE WASHING MACHINE

Put the knitting in a mesh laundry bag and zip it closed. This will stop the knitting from jumping out of the bag and help prevent loose fibers clogging up the filter on the washing machine. Place the bag into the washing machine along with a pair of jeans or an old, lint-free towel to help the felting process. Add a small amount of liquid fabric detergent and set the machine to a full hot cycle (60°C/140°F).

Look through the glass door of the machine every five minutes or so. As soon as the knitted stitches are no longer visible and the fabric looks like commercial felt, spin the water out of the machine. Rinse the knitting thoroughly by hand in cool water and either spin it gently in the machine or roll it up tightly in a towel and squeeze it. Shape the item with your hands and leave it to dry away from direct heat.

FELTING BY HAND

This is easy to do and it is easier to gauge the results than it is with machine felting, though it can take a while for the knitting to fully felt. Simply hand-wash the knitting in hot water with plenty of liquid fabric detergent. Rub and squeeze it and you will start to feel and see the fibers felting together. When it is felted to your satisfaction, rinse, shape, and dry it as for machine felting.

The Tassel Pot and Bobble Pot (Felted Pots Trio, p. 38) are felted in a washing machine to produce a stronger knitted fabric that will hold its shape.

POM-POM MAKING

There are great pom-pom makers available now that make the task really easy. However, the traditional method using two cardboard circles produces an equally effective result.

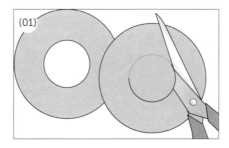

{01}

Cut two cardboard circles with a circle in the center of each one. The diameter of the outer circle will determine the diameter of your pom-pom and that of the inside circle will determine how full the pom-pom will be.

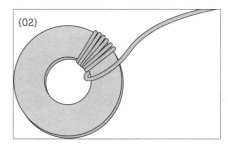

{02}

Hold the two circles together. Wrap yarn around them until the hole in the middle is almost full.

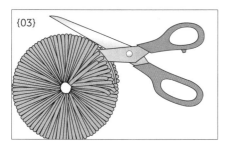

{03}

Using a pair of pointed scissors, cut the yarn around the outside edge of the card circles.

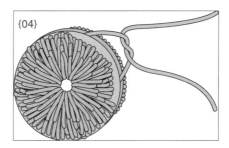

{04}

Wrap a length of yarn tightly around the center of the pom-pom, between the two pieces of card. Tie it as tightly as possible in a knot.

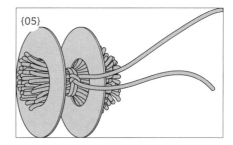

{05}

Slide or cut the cardboard circles off the pom-pom. Fluff the pom-pom up and trim it to an even ball shape with your scissors.

The Pom-pom Headband (p. 18) is topped with a pair of jumbo pom-poms.

INDEX

abbreviations 8

backstitch seam 156
binding off 112–14
blankets, baby 20–3
blocking 153
bobbins 90, 149
bobble hat cushions 48–53
bobbles 131
   bobble pot cover 38–41
bulldog puppy 80–5
burger kitten 66–71

cable cast on 97
cables 127–8
   cable footstool 62–5
cases: intarsia iPad case 58–61
   Swiss darning phone covers 34–7
casting on 95–9
charts 9
Christmas tree decorations 12–15
circular knitting 133–5
circular needles 89, 134–5
color charts 9
color work 136–51
   joining in new colors 140, 150
Continental method 94, 99, 102–3
cushions, bobble hat 48–53

decorations: bulldog puppy 80–5
   Christmas tree 12–15
   kawaii kittens 66–71
   knitted flower bouquet 24–7
   Rudolph the reindeer 54–7
decorative techniques 127–32
decreasing 118–22
double-pointed needles 88, 135
dropped stitches 110
duplicate stitch 139

edges, slip stitch 108
elf tree decoration 12–15
ends, weaving in 152–3
English method 93, 100–1
equipment 90

Fair Isle 140–8
   Fair Isle hot water bottle cover 76–9
felting 157
   felted pot trio 38–41
fingerless mitts, simple lace 31–3

finishing techniques 152–8
flat seam 156
flower bouquet, knitted 24–7
footstool, cable 62–5

garter stitch 104
gauge 6, 10–11

hats: baby hat 20–3
   bobble hat cushions 48–53
headbands, seed stitch 16–19
hot water bottle cover, Fair Isle 76–9

ice cream kitten 66–71
incomplete stitches 110
increasing 115–17
intarsia 149–51
   ends 153
   intarsia diamonds cushion 48–53
   intarsia iPad case 58–61

kawaii kittens 66–71
knit stitch 95, 100, 102
knitting in the round 133–5

lace knitting 129–30
   lacy top socks 72–5
   simple lace fingerless mitts 31–3
loop knitting 132
   loop stitch poncho 42–4

magic loop technique 134
materials 6
mattress stitch 154–6
mistakes, correcting 110

neckwarmer, zigzag 45–7
needles 6, 88–9, 90, 133–5
   holding 93–4

patterns: binding off in 113
   rib patterns 105
patterns, written 6–11
   pattern repeats 9
phone covers, Swiss darning 34–7
pick up and knit 123
pom-poms 158
   pom-pom headband 16–19
poncho, loop stitch 42–4
popcorn kitten 66–71
pot covers, felted 38–41
present tree decoration 12–15
pressing 153

purl stitch 95, 101, 103

reference cards 6
reindeer, Rudolph the 54–7
repeats 7
reverse stockinette stitch 104
ribs 105
Rudolph the reindeer 54–7
rug, tweed stitch 28–30

Santa tree decoration 12–15
Scottish method 93
seams: binding off two edges together 114
   sewing 154–6
seed stitch 106
   seed stitch headbands 16–19
   seed stitch pot cover 38–41
   seed stitch stripy cushion 48–53
shaping knitted pieces 115–26
short-row shaping 124–5
slip knot 96
slipping stitches 108
socks, lacy top 72–5
stitch counts 7
stitches 100–6, 109, 154–6
stockinette stitch 103, 104, 109
stranding yarns 145–8
stripes 136–8
   wide-striped cushion 48–53
Swiss darning 139
   Swiss darning phone covers 34–7

tassel pot cover 38–41
techniques 86–158
through the back loop of a stitch 107
thumb cast on 98
tweed stitch rug 28–30
twisted headband 16–19
twisted stitches 110, 128

unraveling work 111

weaving in ends 152–3
welts 126

yarn 6, 91–2
   bobbins 149
   holding 93–4, 141–4
   joining in a new ball 109

zigzag neckwarmer 45–7

For more information on Mollie Makes please visit www.molliemakes.com

First published in the United States in 2015 by

Interweave
A division of F+W, A Content
+ eCommerce Company
4868 Innovation Drive
Fort Collins, CO 80525

interweave.com

ISBN 978-1-63250-169-1

A CIP catalogue record for this book is available from the British Library.

10 9 8 7 6 5 4 3 2 1

Reproduction by Mission Productions Ltd, Hong Kong
Printed and bound by 1010 Printing International Limited

DABBLE IN CRAFTY GOODNESS WITH MORE *MOLLIE MAKES* BOOKS AVAILABLE FROM INTERWEAVE

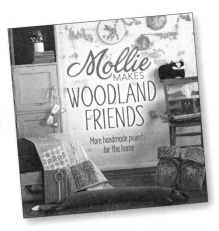

MOLLIE MAKES EMBROIDERY
Adorable Stitched Projects Plus Tips & Tricks
ISBN 978-1-59668-542-0 | $19.99

MOLLIE MAKES WOODLAND FRIENDS
More Handmade Projects for the Home
ISBN: 978-1-62033-540-6 | $12.95

MOLLIE MAKES CROCHET
20+ Cute Projects for the Home Plus Handy Tips and Tricks
ISBN: 978-1-62033-095-1 | $19.95

PUBLISHER'S ACKNOWLEDGMENTS

This book would not have been possible without the input of all our fantastic knitters. We would also like to thank editor Cheryl Brown and designer Sophie Yamamoto. Thanks to Sharon Brant for her expertise in the techniques section, and to Michelle Pickering for her work on the patterns. Thanks to Kuo Kang Chen for the illustrations, Holly Jolliffe for the project photography and Rachel Whiting for the model shots on p43, 46 and 73. Thanks also to Cara Ackerman and DMC Creative World Ltd (www.dmccreative.co.uk) for very generously supplying the Hoooked Zpa-getti yarn, and Coats (www.coats.com) and DMC for providing yarn samples for photography. And of course, thanks to the fantastic team at Mollie Makes for all their help, in particular Lara Watson, Helena Tracey, and Kerry Lawrence.